Garden Tools & Equipment

THE BEST OF
FINE GARDENING®

Garden Tools & Equipment

The Taunton Press

Cover photos: left and bottom, Susan Kahn; top
center, Delilah Smittle; top right, Mark Kane

Back-cover photos: left, Susan Kahn; top right,
Chris Curless; bottom right, Mark Kane

Taunton
BOOKS & VIDEOS
for fellow enthusiasts

First printing: 1995
Printed in the United States of America

A FINE GARDENING Book

FINE GARDENING® is a trademark of The Taunton Press, Inc.,
registered in the U.S. Patent and Trademark Office.

The Taunton Press
63 South Main Street
Box 5506
Newtown, CT 06470-5506

Library of Congress Cataloging-in-Publication Data

Garden tools & equipment.
        p.   cm. — (The Best of Fine gardening)
        Articles originally published in Fine gardening magazine.
        "A Fine gardening book"— T.p. verso.
        Includes index.
        ISBN 1-56158-102-X
        1. Garden tools. 2. Gardening—Equipment and supplies.
        I. Fine gardening. II. Series.
SB454.8.G38   1995   95-10633
635'.9134 — dc20   CIP

Contents

Introduction

Here are the best articles on garden tools and equipment presented by *Fine Gardening* magazine in its first six years of publication.

In this beautifully illustrated collection, expert home gardeners, horticulturists and landscape contractors discuss how to select, use and care for a broad range of gardening aids. Among the articles included, you'll find enlightening profiles of the different types of pruning shears and saws, and of drip and conventional irrigation systems. You'll also find out how to select and use edgings, landscape timbers, and even plant labels to improve your gardening.

This volume is not intended to be a "buyer's guide." The emphasis here is on giving you the right information and perspective to be able to select equipment that fits your own situation, since there really is no one tool that is perfect for everyone. You'll also find lots of good advice about the proper use and care of tools and equipment because, as we all eventually learn, a tool in poor condition or wrongly applied can lead to disastrous results.

The articles in this collection are especially helpful and inspiring because they are the work of enthusiasts who actually use these tools themselves. Sharing their hard-won experience, the authors tell you how to find and use the right tool for your particular needs.

The editors of *Fine Gardening* hope you'll benefit from this book. The more you know about your tools and equipment, the better you'll be able to use them safely and effectively.

"The Best of Fine Gardening" series collects articles from back issues of *Fine Gardening* magazine. A note on p. 96 gives the date of first publication for each article; product availability, suppliers' addresses and prices may have changed since original publication. This book is the eighth in the series.

Digging with Your Wits

You can save your back if you use your head

by Tom Vasale

Many gardeners leap enthusiastically into projects that require digging, but defeat themselves with poor technique or inappropriate tools. Digging doesn't have to be hard on your body. By properly assessing the task, matching the tools to the job and practicing proper digging technique, you can minimize your efforts and save energy for the important part: enjoying your work.

I own a landscape design, installation and maintenance business in Charleston, West Virginia, and my crew and I do a lot of hand digging. Our mountainous topography makes it hard to reach many sites with heavy equipment, and because we work a great deal in established landscapes, we have to be more sensitive than is convenient with large machines.

Before we get started, we identify the task (what does our client want?) and then assess it, determining what we must do to achieve the desired results. These steps, the things we must do, are then reviewed for technique. We call the utility hotline to have any buried wires, gas lines or water pipes located, and then we go to work.

Assessing the task

Different projects require different sorts of digging. In gardening, digging can mean one of three things: digging, pure and simple; shoveling; or spading. Digging turns up, loosens or removes earth. You dig a hole; you dig a drainage ditch; you dig up a plant to be transplanted. Shoveling, on the other hand, moves loose material—soil dug out of a planting hole, for example—from point A to point B. While a hole may be created in the process, the work is limited to the movement of the material. A third process, spading, mixes the material in situ. To improve the soil, we spade compost into soil we've previously dug.

Choosing the right tool

Digging, shoveling and spading require different tools. When we use the wrong tool or try to do everything with just one tool, the work grows harder, tools break and people get injured.

For digging, our tool of choice is the familiar round-point shovel. The point at the tip of the curved blade focuses the digger's weight on a very small area, raising the pounds per square inch and allowing the cutting surface to move through the soil with ease.

The assets of the round-point shovel can also be liabilities. The point can cause the blade to glance off roots and stones, making it twist unexpectedly. In such conditions, we reach for a heavy, square-bladed garden spade. The spade, kept sharp with occasional filing, slices through roots and dislodges small stones.

We do use a rototiller to help dig. The rotating tines break up the soil and allow layers to be shoveled away as we work our way down to the designated depth. When we're down almost as far as we want to go, we loosen the soil at the bottom of the hole with

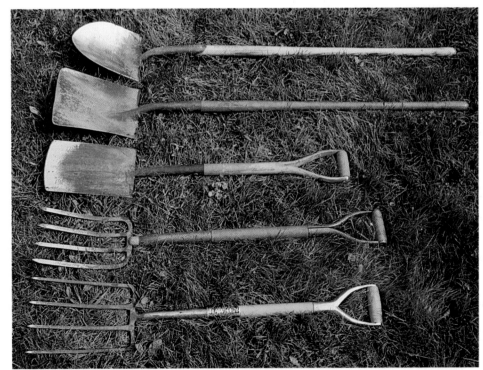

Gravity does the work. Taking full advantage of gravity, a gardener pushes the handle of a round-point shovel away from her so the blade cuts straight down into the edge of a new flower bed. Good digging technique makes the job easier.

Different tools for different work. The standard arsenal of digging tools might include (from top to bottom) a round-point shovel, a square-point shovel, a garden spade, a flat-tined spading fork and a square-tined digging fork.

All photos: Susan Kahn

Moving material from here to there. A gardener returns soil to a planting bed using a square-point shovel, lifting with her legs, not her back. The square-point shovel is ideally suited to shoveling loose materials from flat surfaces such as a tarp.

Less is more. A slice of turf and soil from the side of a planting hole adheres to the blade of a round-point shovel. Although taking slices appears to under-utilize the capacity of a shovel, slices are easier to cut and lift than heavy chunks.

Good and bad digging technique compared

There is more to digging than grabbing a tool and getting started. By paying attention to good technique, you can save yourself an aching back.

Bad technique
Lifting soil while your knees are locked forces you to bend at the waist, making your back muscles do the work.

A fully loaded shovel taxes the tool and the gardener.

Good technique

By keeping your back straight and bending your knees as you lift, you do the work with your leg muscles and spare your back.

A slice taken from the side of the hole can be lifted with ease.

a digging fork to promote drainage (the rotating tines of the rototiller tend to close soil pores in our clay). Gardeners fortunate enough to have lighter soil can skip this step.

For shoveling, we use one of two tools. To move loose material resting on a flat surface, we prefer a square-point, flat-backed shovel like those used by construction workers. The large head holds more material than that of the round-point shovel. And the flat back slides easily over driveways or a tarp where we've piled material to make clean-up easier. For shoveling soil out of planting holes, we use the round-point shovel because its smaller head fits into tight spaces.

For spading, I prefer what tool manufacturers call a digging fork, which looks like a short-handled pitchfork with sturdy, square tines. I've tried flat-tined spading forks, but the outer tines tend to bend back under the weight of our heavy clay. Some of my employees prefer the round-point shovel for spading. It works well when the soil is dry or just a little damp, but I find our clay builds up more on the shovel than it does on the fork, adding unnecessary weight.

Combining tasks and tools

My crew and I often use all three digging methods and a variety of tools in the same project. Soil preparation is a good example. Our soil ranges from heavy clay to heavier clay, requiring a lot of digging to prepare it for planting. To amend the soil, we add large quantities of organic matter, such as compost or manure, and dig it as deep as 30 in. into the soil.

When excavating to such depths, the rototiller comes in handy, but it digs just 6 in. deep. If we're preparing a 24-in. deep bed, we have to remove 18 in. of soil before we can till the bottom 6 in. of soil. Do we dig it out? No way! We till the top 6 in., shovel the loose soil aside with square-point shovels, till the next 6 in., shovel that out of the hole, repeat the process once more and end up with a huge hole 18 in. deep. After loosening another 6 in. of soil—that makes 24 in. all together—we throw in one-quarter of the compost and spade it into the soil with forks or shovels. Then we replace each layer of soil we removed—in order—and amend it with compost.

If you're preparing a small garden bed or digging a planting hole for a small shrub, you can do without a tiller. The round-point shovel and the

Proper spading technique

By following proper spading technique, you can turn the soil without giving yourself a sore back.

With the aid of gravity, plunge the fork down into the soil.

Push the handle down until the tines pop up.

Then, keeping your back straight, lift the fork with your legs and turn the soil over.

fork do the job just fine. And if your soil is easier to work and drains better than our clay, you may not need to prepare the soil as deep as we do. Many gardeners get good results with beds dug just 8 in. to 10 in. deep.

Digging smart

There is more to digging, shoveling and spading than grabbing a shovel or a fork and putting your muscles to work. Digging is not simply a physical task—if you use your brain and follow good digging technique, you can save yourself time, energy, and wear and tear on your body.

Digging is easiest if you let gravity do most of the work. Gravity pulls straight down, so you'll get the most help from it if you dig straight down. Pay attention to the angle at which you hold the shovel. If the handle is straight up and down, the blade isn't, and you're wasting energy. Push the handle away from you until the blade is vertical. Then add your weight to the shovel by stepping on it.

Once you've lifted out that first shovelful, limit your work to taking thin slices of soil from the sides of the hole. A fully loaded shovel strains backs and tires muscles. It also stresses tools. Anything more than a slice has to be pried away from the side of the hole. Shovel handles are for lifting, not prying. Smart diggers have learned

that a medium-weight slice of soil is easy to cut and lift, yet substantial enough to hang together on the blade until it's brought up out of the hole.

Lift a loaded shovel with your legs, not your back. Leg and arm muscles are strong; back muscles are comparatively weak. If you keep your back straight and bend your knees, you transfer the effort of lifting to your stronger leg muscles, decreasing the risk of back injury. But old habits are hard to break. I still catch myself pushing the shovel in with my back straight, lifting the full shovel—knees locked—as I straighten up. Having once injured my back, I should know better.

Shoveling material that's already loose—sand, compost, prepared soil—requires a different stance. While digging harnesses the downward force of gravity, shoveling is a horizontal movement. Hold the shovel so its back is on the ground and push it into the pile. Push from the end of the handle, not from the side. Pushing from the end lets your weight do the work. Once the shovel is loaded, bend your knees—not your back—and lift the load.

Spading soil amendments into loosened soil requires techniques similar to those used in digging. Plunge the fork or round-point shovel straight down into the soil, then lift and turn the soil with your back straight and your knees bent. Using the spading tool as a lever

is the easiest way to begin lifting. I pull the handle toward me, push it down to the ground, and up comes the soil. Then I slide one hand forward, shifting my weight from my rear foot to my forward foot with my knees still bent, lift the head of the tool slightly, using my legs, and turn it over.

Whatever sort of digging you do, it's important to pace yourself so you don't get exhausted. Exhausted workers trip over their own feet, drop loads and develop sloppy work habits. Before fatigue sets in, take occasional brief breaks. Leaning on your shovel now and then is not a sign of laziness. It's a great way to appreciate the portion of the job completed while drinking a glass of water.

Digging is one of the pleasures of gardening. Get some good tools, choose the pace and posture that's right for you and enjoy your work while you dream about the difference you're making in your landscape. If it's still too cold or the soil is too damp to begin your digging project today, go for your daily walk instead. Walking is the best way to prepare your body for the season ahead. □

Tom Vasale is a horticulturist and the owner of Tom's Word Horticulture Consulting, a landscape design, installation and maintenance business in Charleston, West Virginia.

A brush and a stream of water scour a shovel blade caked with mud. Routine cleaning, oiling and sharpening make hand tools work better and last longer.

Caring for Hand Tools

How to keep them solid, clean and sharp

by Sandy Snyder

When I began gardening, it didn't occur to me that I needed to know how to care for tools. I had a hus-band to do that. So I was up-set when my husband de-cided that I should learn to care for my own tools. I wanted to garden, not spend my time cleaning, sharpening and oiling prun-ing shears and shovels. Any-way, I asked myself, why bother caring for tools when new ones are inexpensive and readily available?

Since then I've learned that good tools are worth preserving. They're not cheap and not so easy to find. Over my many years of gardening, first as an am-ateur and now as a profes-sional gardener at the Den-ver Botanic Gardens, I've been through a lot of tools. It took a long time to find cutting and digging tools that are the right size, heft and fit for me. I can't afford to neglect them and then throw them away, so I've learned to take care of them. I even enjoy it.

Cleaning and oiling

Dirty, rusty tools make gardening more difficult. Pruning shears and loppers get gummed up with sap and cut badly. Shovels cake with mud and become heavy. When your tools perform poorly, you have to work harder. They are slow to cut through stems, soil or roots, and they take a toll on your muscles and hands.

You can save yourself exasperation and effort if you clean your tools every time you use them. For most tools, cleaning is simple. Wash off the dirt and dry the tool with a rag. Then, wipe the metal parts with oil or spray them with a petroleum-based lubricant and rust inhibitor, such as WD-40, which is widely available at hardware stores, as are the other supplies I use.

To remove sap and dirt from cutting tools, such as pruning shears and loppers, or to clean dried mud from shovels and spades, I use a medium-coarse wire wheel on an electric bench grinder. If you don't want to invest in a grinder, you can clean tools by hand with a wire brush or a wire brush attachment for an electric drill. Emery cloth, a gritty, sandpaper-like material available in fine, medium and coarse grades, also works well.

Pruning saws also get clogged with sap and sawdust. I clean saws with mineral spirits (a solvent) and then apply a film of oil or WD-40 to keep rust at bay.

Wooden handles need care, too. If moisture works its way into the wood, it can cause splitting and splintering, so wash mud off handles after every use and then dry them well. On occasion, wipe handles down with a rag moistened with boiled linseed oil; the oil helps seal the wood where varnish has worn away.

A spinning wire brush removes clinging dirt from a shovel blade. Wire brushes, along with other cleaning and sharpening tools, are available at hardware stores.

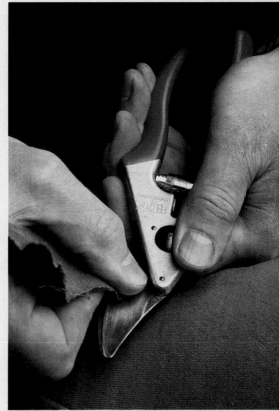

Emery cloth, a flexible, cloth-backed abrasive that can work into tight spaces, takes sap and dirt off a pair of shears.

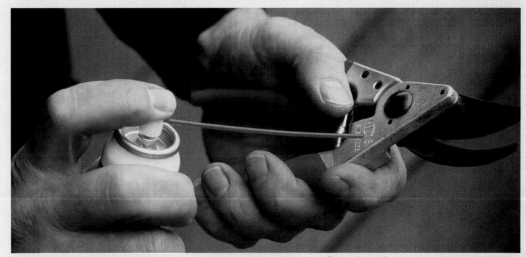

After cleaning, coat metal parts with oil or an aerosol lubricant such as WD-40 (shown above) to reduce friction between moving parts and prevent rust.

Protect wooden handles as shown here by rubbing them with boiled linseed oil to prevent the swelling and cracking that water can cause.

Keeping a sharp edge

A ceramic whetstone with a triangular cross-section handily sharpens the entire blade of a pair of shears, from the tip down into the narrow throat.

A diamond sharpener, such as the one shown here, has a patch of diamond grit glued to a plastic handle. The handle is thin enough to allow you to sharpen shears easily without disassembling them.

Shears and loppers cut better and damage plants less if they're sharp. Once or twice a year, I take mine apart and sharpen them with a motorized whetstone I bought at a large hardware store. A whetstone attachment for a bench grinder or electric drill is just as effective. So is a fine-toothed file that removes a small amount of metal. For occasional light honing without disassembling the tool, I use a three-sided ceramic stone made by Felco (available at garden centers that carry Felco products). You can also use a diamond sharpener, which has diamond grit glued to a handle.

To sharpen a blade by hand, hold the file, ceramic stone or diamond sharpener at a slight angle to the cutting edge and push it away from the blade. (This action is shown on a spade in the drawing at the top of the facing page.) Repeat this one-way motion all along the blade, checking sharpness occasionally by cutting a piece of paper. Sharpening one side of a blade creates a slight burr (a small ridge of metal) on the other side. Remove the burr with a few light passes almost flat to the blade.

Pruning and lopping shears aren't the only tools that benefit from sharpening. A garden spade cuts through soil and roots much more easily if it's sharp. It doesn't need a razor's edge. Use a file or an electric grinder with a coarse stone to remove nicks and put a slight edge on the blade.

Salvaging neglected tools

A sanding disc in an electric drill (left) removes metal from a spade to smooth rust pits. Coarse sandpaper, such as the 80-grit paper shown below, quickly removes all but the deepest pockets of rust. A close look at the blade midway through cleaning (right) shows how effectively the sanding disc polishes the steel.

Spades work better when sharp. A close-up of a blade before sharpening (above) shows a nicked and rounded edge capable of cutting through sod and roots only with great effort. Several passes with a bastard mill file (above right) give a bright, clean edge (below right) that will cut with less effort and yet resist wear and nicks.

Detail

File

Blade

File tip

Heel of the file

How to sharpen a spade

Holding the file at a slight angle as shown in detail above, push the file from tip to heel away from the blade, while sweeping from one side of the blade to the other.

Neglected tools can often be salvaged. Renew rusted and pitted shovels, hoes or pruning shears with the same tools you use for regular cleaning: a wire brush or emery cloth. You can also remove rust with a sanding disc attachment for an electric drill. If the metal is corroded or nicked beyond repair, you may be able to buy replacement parts from a hardware store or a garden center, or by writing directly to the manufacturer. Replacement handles may also be available.

The heads of some tools are attached to the handle by a tang, an extension of

the steel head that fits inside the wood. If the wood shrinks away from the tang, the head spins around or falls off. I use an epoxy glue to put these parts back together. A gardening friend swears by a product called Chair-Loc, available at hardware stores. Chair-Loc is a liquid that makes wood swell. You pour it into the hole in the handle so the wood grips the tang. □

Sandy Snyder is a gardener in the Rock Alpine Garden at Denver Botanic Gardens, Denver, Colorado. Clean, sharp tools make her work easier.

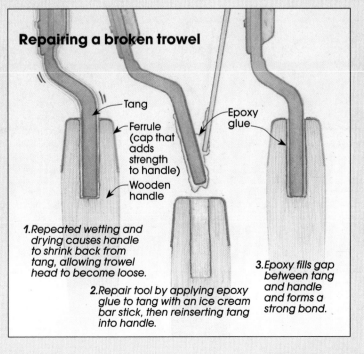

Repairing a broken trowel

Tang

Ferrule (cap that adds strength to handle)

Epoxy glue

Wooden handle

1. Repeated wetting and drying causes handle to shrink back from tang, allowing trowel head to become loose.

2. Repair tool by applying epoxy glue to tang with an ice cream bar stick, then reinserting tang into handle.

3. Epoxy fills gap between tang and handle and forms a strong bond.

Illustrations: Gary Williamson

Digging Tools
A good tool, kept sharp, makes a difference

by Tom Vasale

I've supervised as few as one and as many as 86 employees in my career as a horticulturist in Charleston, West Virginia, so I've had the chance to watch a lot of people using and abusing hand tools. I've seen the shortcomings of cheap tools and developed a respect for good-quality ones, and I'd like to pass along some tips on se-

lecting and maintaining two tools I, like most gardeners, depend on: the spade and the digging fork. (I use the words "shovel" and "spade" interchangeably, but for clarity, I'll stick with spade in this article.)

It's important to match the tool to the job—even a well-made tool won't give satisfaction if it's not right for the task or conditions. I specialize in designing and installing herbaceous perennial beds and borders, and I'm most often working on clay soil. West Virginia has yellow clay, brown clay, and a red clay that's best de-scribed as "greasy." Clay drains poorly,

and can shrink and swell dramatically with fluctuating moisture levels. Ground that's too slick to stand on in the spring may be a mosaic of baked soil and gap-ing cracks by August. Even in the deep woods of the Appalachians, this area of the country has the thinnest topsoil I've ever seen. Around newly constructed

Used daily in heavy clay soils, sturdy, well-main-tained tools like those above give Vasale years of service. From left are a square-point garden spade with a Y-D grip, a round-point spade, and a heavy-duty digging fork with square tines.

Drawings: Laura B. Goodwin

houses, where lots have been scraped and graded, there may be no topsoil at all.

I don't use a rototiller, because it works the soil only 6 in. to 12 in. deep, and it compacts the clay at that depth into a dense, impermeable layer that hinders drainage and root penetration. I think double-digging to 24 in. deep with hand tools is a better way to prepare beds, especially for long-term plantings, because it provides plants with a deep volume of fertile, moisture-retentive, rapidly draining soil.

The handles of our forks and spades take a lot of stress, especially if we're working soil that's been fallow for a while or is compacted. I prefer wooden handles, and look for those with straight, fine grain. With proper care, a wooden handle won't splinter, and it will break only if abused. When one does break, it can be replaced, and around here almost any hardware store that sells replacement handles will install them for a modest charge. Because of the slight risk of hitting an underground wire in a landscaped area, we avoid metal handles on digging tools. They're terribly cold in the winter, as well, and damp gloves stick to them annoyingly.

Before buying a spade or a fork, I look to see how the handle is attached. Wooden handles are tapered to fit snugly into a matching socket forged or welded as a single unit with the tool's head. (Cheap forks often have two-piece heads—a tang on the tines fits into a hole in the handle, which is sheathed in a metal casing.) Some have a thick bolt or metal pin that runs sideways through the socket to keep the handle in place. Because this runs perpendicular to the pressure applied when you're moving soil, it constitutes a weak spot where I've seen handles break. All other things being equal, I prefer tools with a thin, tight-fitting pin that passes from front to back, not side to side.

I also look at the socket itself. If a metal socket is open at the bottom or along the back, soil and moisture can get caught inside and be held against the wooden handle. This will cause the wood to rot, particularly if the tool is stored in a damp area. I think this is the reason for many of the broken-handled spades I see at garage sales. Closed-back spades and those sold as "solid socket" avoid this problem.

For moving a pile of soil, my helpers choose a short-handled spade with a "Y-D" grip. The short handle makes it easy for the user to bend over, scoop and move the soil in a smooth, continuous motion. Long-handled spades offer more leverage for digging the upper layer of a double-dug bed, but a long handle is more apt to break if someone tries to use the spade as a pry-bar.

We sand any varnish or similar finish off new wooden handles, as varnish is likely to flake off, leaving checks and

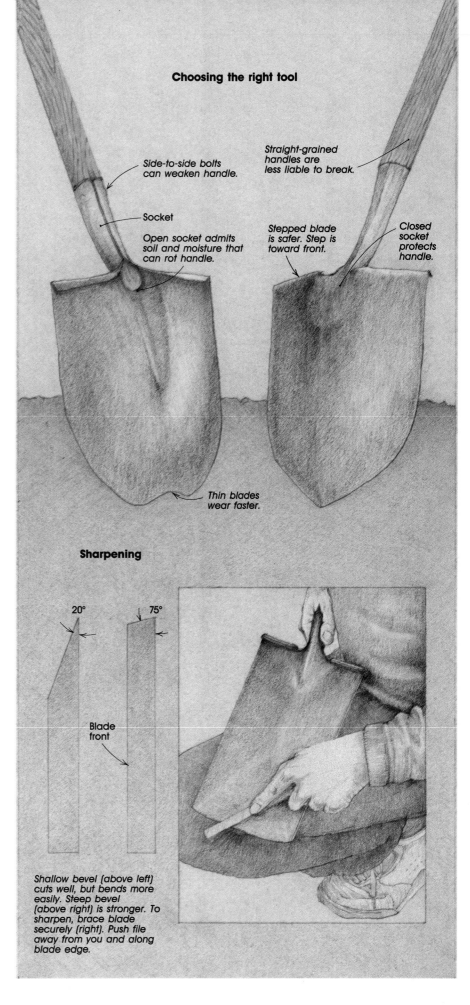

Choosing the right tool

Side-to-side bolts can weaken handle.

Straight-grained handles are less liable to break.

Socket

Open socket admits soil and moisture that can rot handle.

Stepped blade is safer. Step is toward front.

Closed socket protects handle.

Thin blades wear faster.

Sharpening

20°   75°

Blade front

Shallow bevel (above left) cuts well, but bends more easily. Steep bevel (above right) is stronger. To sharpen, brace blade securely (right). Push file away from you and along blade edge.

cracks that can lead to splinters. Instead, we finish the wood with a few coats of boiled linseed oil, which soaks into the wood and doesn't wear off. (Be sure to buy boiled, not raw, linseed oil.) We sand and re-oil our wooden tool handles about twice a year—a good rainy-day job. If a handle becomes loose with age as the wood dries out and shrinks, I buy a little glycerin at the drugstore and pour it down the socket. The glycerin causes the wood to swell and doesn't evaporate. I learned this trick from a piano tuner, who used it on a neighbor's piano to tighten the pegs in the wooden soundboard.

The blades of lightweight metal spades wear down quickly and bend out of shape. When I was director of the city of Charleston's Beautification Department, I supervised crews of hired laborers. We couldn't justify buying top-quality tools— we were liable to lose them—but when the crews used cheap spades to dig in the gravelly soil along roadsides, the rounded blades would become blunt and eventually even concave. Heavy-gauge metal spades serve indefinitely, as they don't wear down. Also, all the spades I purchase have turned-back steps at the top of the blade. Stepless digging tools are hazardous—they'll cut deeply into your leg if your foot slips off.

My employees prefer the Ames heavy-duty, solid-shank, round-point spade for most digging, perhaps because they're used to it. (Listed as a shovel, it costs about $40 from A.M. Leonard, Inc., 6665 Spiker Rd., Piqua, OH 45356; catalog free.) It's good for starting a hole, since your weight and leverage all lean on the center point, and it's good for moving a pile of soil. I prefer Smith & Hawken's heavy-duty garden spade (about $43 from Smith & Hawken, 25 Corte Madera, Mill Valley, CA 94941; catalog free). It's a square-point tool, so I can cut a slice of soil, lean back and lift it out of the hole in a single stroke. With a round-point spade, a lot of the soil falls off the edge and back down into the hole, and then you have to scoop it out. Of course, any soil will crumble some as you dig, but you can use a square-point spade as a broom for sweeping up the loose soil at the bottom of a hole.

Nothing beats a good fork for mixing amendments into the soil. We use forks to work both the bottom and top layers of double-dug beds, to thoroughly blend the various components of the soil mix and create a loose, open texture. No spading fork we've tried has ever stood up to our heavy soil. Spading forks have tines that are wider than they are thick. The outer tines, especially, bend after prolonged use, and you can reposition them only so many times before they'll break. Smith & Hawken sells what they call a garden fork,

which has thick tines that are square instead of flat. (These tools cost from about $43 to $47.) The square tines are incomparably sturdy—they don't bend. We've used one of these forks since 1980 and the tines are still in their original positions.

Exposure to water and air will cause steel and iron tools to rust. The heads of often-used spades and forks rarely need much attention, as digging keeps them smooth, polished and rust-free. Seldom-used digging tools, or those being stored for the winter, can be wire-brushed and greased, but I've found that it's quicker to protect them by plunging the heads up and down in a bucket filled with coarse builders' sand and a little motor oil. Any sand adhering to the heads after this treatment can be brushed off with a whisk broom. With this care, a good forged-steel head wears well, and I don't see a need for more costly stainless-steel tools.

Sharpening

Digging forks don't need to be sharpened, but a spade works best with a beveled edge on the blade. To understand the role of sharpening, think a little about what actually happens when a spade moves through the soil. As you push down on the spade, your weight is concentrated on the cutting edge. The pounds per square inch of pressure exerted against the soil is a function of your downward thrust divided by the square inches of surface area on the cutting edge of the blade. If that blade is sharp, the cutting edge is thin, so the pressure per square inch increases, making your job go easier. If that sounds confusing, let's put it into practice.

I weighed 200 lb. this morning. My square-point garden spade has a blade 7 in. wide at the cutting edge. The steel from which it's forged is about 1/8 in. thick at the edge right now (it's dull!). That means that if I just step down on the spade, without any jumping about, the pressure at the edge will be about 229 lb. per sq. in. (200 divided by 7/8 sq. in.).

If I put a bevel on the front side of that blade, reducing the metal at the edge to about 1/64 in. thick, my 200 lb. would be concentrated on just 7/64 sq. in. That's 1,829 lb. per sq. in., an eightfold increase. A lot of this pressure is expended against the friction of the soil on the blade as it moves into the earth—digging is still hard work even when a tool is sharp. But the sharpening helps.

I mentioned above that the bevel is on the front side of the blade. This is important. As pressure is exerted down on the sharpened edge, it's exerted out on the bevel. If the bevel is on the front, it keeps the spade in line and forces the soil up onto the blade. With the bevel on the back, the soil would crumble off, so you would have to dig at it twice to get it out of the hole, and the spade wouldn't

go where you wanted it to.

The exact angle of the sharpened bevel isn't critical. A shallow angle cuts more easily, but the thin metal is liable to bend. A steep bevel angle is stronger, but harder to push through the soil. There's a happy medium that evolves for each person and each kind of job. Our light-duty spades get about a 20° bevel. Heavy-duty tree spades are maintained at a 70° or 75° bevel because a thinner edge would bend when we chopped at roots.

More important than the degree of the angle is the constancy of the angle across the blade. All blades wear down, and they do so first at the thinnest points. If a blade is sharpened unevenly, with a long-tapered bevel in one place and a blunt bevel in another, the thinner spots will wear out first. To make an even bevel along a blade, I try to hold the tool as solidly as possible while sharpening it. I may feel like a contortionist, bracing the tool against my leg and a tree or other object while trying to leave my hands free to do the work. But if the tool were to wobble, I'd end up with a sloppy job.

I like a 7-in., single-cut, "garden" or "bastard" file (sold by Sears or most hardware stores) for field sharpening. It fits easily in my back pocket and doesn't clog with metal filings or soil. Unlike a sharpening stone, metal files won't break if dropped. A single-cut file cuts only in one direction. Hold it so that it cuts when pushed away from you. The tool being sharpened should point away from you, too, so that the file is being pushed off the blade, not onto it. Pushing the file off the blade draws the blade to a finer point. For the best cut, lay the teeth of the file at a 90° angle to the blade and push the file forward along its axis. It's sort of a push-forward-while-moving-to-the-side action that glides the file across the edge of the tool while moving the file forward at the same time.

Sharpening creates a "burr." This is the very thinnest part of the sharpened blade—so thin that as the blade is sharpened, it bends around to the back. You should remove the burr by turning the tool over and lightly filing the back edge. Place the file almost flat along the back of the tool, and make one or two passes.

I didn't sharpen my tools very often when I first started out, but after doing so a few times, I grew to appreciate the ease of working with a properly sharpened spade. The people who work for me notice a difference, too, and the sharp tools are always the first ones grabbed when there's a choice. When you're working in your own garden, you'll find another advantage to sharpening periodically: It gives you time to pause and admire your work. □

Tom Vasale is a horticultural consultant in Charleston, West Virginia.

A homeowner rakes leaves into the MacKissic/Mighty Mac Leaf Shredder-Chipper. The shredder can be used upright or lying on the ground. Shredded leaves collect in a cloth bag.

Leaf Shredders
New generation of machines for gardeners

by Renée Beaulieu

The national trend towards banning yard waste from municipal landfills has helped gardeners: more manufacturers are making machines sized for homeowners that shred leaves and chip brush, making it easier to com-

post or otherwise dispose of yard debris. A shredder can help you turn a potential waste into a resource that will enrich your garden. Hardware stores, garden centers, chain outlets and mail-order catalogs now carry a variety of chipper-shredders.

Shredders cut large leaves into small pieces, thus reducing their volume. Shredded leaves compost faster than whole ones. They can make a better mulch than whole leaves do, be-

cause they are less likely to create a solid mat that keeps water from penetrating the soil. As leaves break down, they turn a nice neutral brown.

I have an abundance of leaves in my yard and wanted to use them as mulch, so I sampled seven leaf shredders available for homeowners with a range of prices and features. I tried electric and gasoline-powered models. Some had a top-loading hopper into which leaves are dumped;

Photo: Renée Beaulieu

in others, the leaves are raked into the machine at ground level. Several machines also vacuumed the leaves.

Different capabilities

The price and capabilities of shredders vary considerably. I tried models that range in price from about $100 to over $1,000. Some consume only leaves. Others can take twigs and stems of herbaceous plants. Most shredders can also chip branches, sometimes as big as 3½ in. in diameter. However, leaf shredders aren't necessarily designed to also shred large quantities of tough, fibrous garden debris. Shredders designed for home use take more time to do a job than the big, more expensive commercial grinders do.

To use most shredders, you rake up piles of leaves and move the shredder from pile to pile, usually shutting it off for the move. Many have wheels to make moving easier. Shredder-vacs take over some or all of the lifting and raking—you push them like a lawn mower, and they suck up leaves. All of the shredders I tried had separate, small chutes for feeding branches directly to the blades. Those I tried with electric motors start with a simple on-off switch, but they require long, grounded extension cords designed for outdoor use. You can move them only as far as the cord permits. Gasoline-powered machines are more mobile, but require more routine maintenance.

Most of the shredders had catch-bags—large, cloth bags that collect the shredded leaves. The usual capacity of the bags was 3¼ to 3½ bushels. Some machines won't start unless the bag is in place; others will, but I wouldn't want to use them without the bag, because the leaves are blown out with such force.

It's best to shred leaves when they're dry. You can shred wet leaves, but they form sticky clumps that can jam cutting blades or the throat of the hopper. To shred them, you must slow down the rate of feeding or toss in handfuls of dry material to clear the machine's throat.

Electric shredders

The Electric Leaf-Eater LE-900 by Flowtron just shreds leaves. Retailing at $119.99, it was the least expensive model I tested. (For information about purchasing shredders, see Sources on facing page.) Basically a string-trimmer mounted inside a plastic drum, it has two doubled, nylon strings whirling around. You feed leaves into the top

of a drum that is open at both ends and is attached to a cantilevered stand. You can put a trash can, plastic bag or tarp underneath the drum to catch the shredded leaves. The opening at the bottom of the hopper is adjustable, changing the size of leaf pieces from coarse to fine.

If twigs are mixed in with the leaves, they will snap the nylon trimmer lines. The oak leaves I shredded had plenty of twigs mixed in, and I had to replace the string approximately every half hour. But the procedure takes only a minute or so.

A gardener prepares to drop a big handful of leaves into a Flowtron Electric Leaf-Eater. Many shredders have a similar design, in which leaves are lifted into a hopper and collected in a bag on the way out.

When working alone, I found the Leaf-Eater was efficient, but two people feeding leaves into the machine at the same time tended to overload it. A circuit breaker shuts the motor off before it burns out, but if you get a whiff of burning electrical insulation, don't ignore it: turn the shredder off and let it cool down. When you resume, slow down the rate at which you're feeding it and maybe adjust to a coarser grind.

Flowtron also makes an electric shredder—the Chipper Shredder Mulcher CS3500. With steel knives, it shreds

leaves and twigs and can also chip branches up to 2½ in. in diameter. The plastic hopper narrows and curves at the bottom, a design that ensures safety because it's physically impossible to put your fingers into the blades. But unplug it to clear jams anyway. The CS3500 comes with a plastic pusher stick that helps you push leaves through the curve at the bottom of the hopper, if necessary. Sprinkling an armload in by handfuls rather than all at once meant a smoother operation. This approach meant that shredding took longer than with the Leaf-Eater, but the Chipper Shredder Mulcher can take twigs mixed with leaves. It also can be tipped onto its side so you can rake directly into it instead of lifting leaves up into the hopper.

Gasoline-powered shredders

I tried two 5-hp gas-powered shredders. Both have bags to catch leaves, can grind twigs along with the leaves without jamming, and have separate chutes for chipping larger branches. The Simplicity 5C Chipper/Shredder has a top-loading leaf hopper, but you can also buy a flexible vacuum hose for it. The MacKissic/Mighty Mac Leaf Shredder-Chipper LSC505 can be used either upright or tipped to the ground so leaves can be raked into it. The gas tank remains sealed and safe whether the unit is upright or laid down.

The Simplicity produced the most consistently finely shredded leaves of any model I tested. I tried the vacuum attachment, which has two interchangeable nozzles. One is a flat scoop that lies on the ground while you rake into it. The other, about 6 in. in diameter and held by a metal pole, can be used to suck leaves out of a pile or a window well or out of ground covers without damaging them.

The MacKissic can be used in an upright position, or you can tip it and rake into it. The raking pace was very comfortable—no excruciating pain in the shoulders, and mounds of leaves disappeared quickly. Raking was faster than lifting leaves up to the hopper.

At 3 hp, the Yardvark by Kemp Company is smaller than the other gasoline-powered shredders I tried, making it lighter and easier to push up and down sloping ground. With a change of attachments, the Yardvark becomes a leaf-blower on wheels, a vacuum or a shredder. It can grind twigs with the leaves without jamming and has a separate chute for chipping branches up to 1½-in. in diameter.

Because the outer edge of the collecting bag unzips, it's possible to empty it without detaching it, although as a precaution, you still should stop the machine first as the leaves spew out with great force while the machine is running.

The Yardvark has excellent safety features—the engine automatically shuts down when any attachment is removed, including the bag. This shredder can also be partially disassembled to take less room for long-term storage.

Leaf vacuums

Machines designed to pick up, shred and bag leaves are the newest entry in the shredder market. They look like oversized lawn mowers—you push the machines, and they vacuum up the leaves from your lawn. I tried models in two sizes.

Garden Way's 4-hp Chipper/Vac is designed for properties of a half acre or less. The leading edge is a downward-facing slot, which can be replaced with a ledge so you can rake leaves into it rather than vacuuming them up. I found the slot needed unclogging frequently, especially on a lawn littered with twigs. There is also a small chute for chipping branches up to 1½ in. in diameter. The Chipper/Vac is for clearing fairly flat lawns, although you can buy a vacuum attachment to clear uneven areas.

Troy-Bilt's Chipper/Vac, retailing for $1,399, was the biggest and most expensive unit I tried. At 5 hp, it is self-propelled and designed for properties from a half to two acres, probably best suited to those with a big lawn. It's heavy, so the self-propelling feature was very useful. It was the only shredder I tried that had a transmission. A wide, built-in nozzle snuffed up leaves, small twigs and even hickory nuts. It's designed so you can walk beside it and feed larger twigs into the hopper without pausing. There's a chute for branches up to 3½ in. in diameter. You can buy a vacuum hose attachment to reach uneven areas. The bag is big and can be unzipped for emptying. A 4-hp Chipper/Vac that needs pushing is also available.

Safety first

Most of the models I tried are designed to prevent accidents and have safety features that would be hard to bypass. But I still treated the machines with the respect reserved for any potentially dangerous tools.

Leaf shredders vary in size, price and features. Clockwise from lower left: the Simplicity 5C Chipper/Shredder, Garden Way Chipper/Vac, Troy-Bilt Chipper/Vac, Flowtron Electric Leaf-Eater, Flowtron Chipper Shredder Mulcher, Kemp's Yardvark, with the MacKissic /Mighty Mac Leaf Shredder-Chipper in the center.

SOURCES

Except for the Yardvark, the shredders listed are sold locally. Call customer service numbers provided for a nearby retailer. Prices are manufacturers' suggested retail prices.

- Flowtron **Electric Leaf-Eater** (LE-900), 8-amp electric motor, $119.99. Flowtron Outdoor Products, 2 Main St.., Melrose, MA 02146, 1-800-343-3280. Flowtron **Chipper Shredder Mulcher** (CS3500), 12-amp motor, $349. Address, phone, above.

- Garden Way **Chipper/Vac,** 4 hp., $499, Garden Way Inc., 102nd St.. and 9th Ave., Troy, NY 12180, 1-800-437-8686.

- Kemp's **Yardvark,** 3 hp, $694, is sold direct by Kemp Co., 160 Koser Rd., Lititz, PA 17543-9988. 1-800-441-5367.

- MacKissic/**Mighty Mac Leaf Shredder-Chipper** (LSC505) 5 hp, $569. MacKissic Inc., P.O. Box 111, Parker Ford, PA 19457, 215-495-7181.

- Simplicity **5C Chipper/Shredder,** 5 hp, $599. Simplicity Manufacturing Inc., 500 North Spring Street, P.O. Box 997, Port Washington, WI 53074-0997, 1-800-945-0235.

- Troy-Bilt **Chipper/Vac;** 5 hp, $1,399. Troy-Bilt Manufacturing Co., 102nd St. and 9th Avenue, Troy, NY 12180, 1-800-437-8686.

Take these simple precautions, and take them seriously. The manufacturer's safety guidelines are intended to protect the user. Read about them in the owner's manual, which also contains important details about your machine's operation.

Keep your hands away from the blades; they're powerful enough to cause serious damage. Wear gloves and safety glasses or goggles while using a shredder. On electric shredders, use a heavy-duty, grounded extension cord rated for outdoor use and for your machine's capacity. Before trying to unclog jammed leaves or to service the machine, turn it off; disconnect the spark plug on gas-powered models, the power plug on electric ones.

Wear earplugs—these machines are loud enough to damage hearing after prolonged exposure. You don't need those big industrial earmuffs; the soft foam ear plugs sold at drug or hardware stores work just fine. Electric motors are quieter than gasoline engines, but you should protect your ears when using them, too. □

Renée Beaulieu likes to use shredded oak leaves as a mulch for her perennial garden in Waterbury, Connecticut.

Pruning Shears
The right pair fits your hands and needs

by Chris Curless

With so many kinds of pruning shears on the market, how do you choose the pair best suited to your needs and budget? In search of the answer, I looked at 64 models, the ones you're most likely to find in a garden center, hardware store or mail-order catalog. Rather than include specialty items such as bonsai snips, I looked only at general-purpose shears capable of cutting woody branches up to ½ in. in diameter. I spoke to the manufacturers, examined their technical information and then used the shears in my backyard. Here's some of what I learned.

Two classes of pruning shears

There are two main classes of pruning shears: bypass and anvil. Bypass shears work like scissors, except that only the upper half is a blade. The lower half—usually referred to as the hook—is a blunt-edged, curved piece of metal that cradles the stem, preventing it from sliding while the blade cuts through it. The blade is flat on the side next to the hook and beveled on the other side.

Anvil shears work like a knife on a cutting board. The blade closes on a flat piece, usually made of a relatively soft metal such as brass or aluminum, called the anvil. A soft metal yields slightly to the steel blade, allowing the blade to hold its edge longer. The blade is ground in the shape of a wedge, sharpened on both sides.

Each class of pruning shears has its advantages. Bypass pruning shears, properly used, cause less damage to the stem than anvil shears do. The hook digs into the branch, but the damage is on the part of the branch you remove. On anvil shears, the anvil tends to crush the bark on both sides of the cut. However, while anvil shears as a group do more damage than bypass shears, the damage varies from model to model. In my hands, the Sandvik P38-20, Rolcut 50, Fiskars 4103, Wallace P15T and Wallace P21H did hardly any damage at all.

Bypass shears have other advantages. The thin tip of most bypass models makes it possible to get the jaws into tight spots. And bypass shears allow you to cut a branch at the spot that leaves the parent plant least susceptible to infection and decay at the wound. If the blade, not the hook, is nearest the parent branch as shown in the lower left photograph on the facing page, you can prune a side branch at the ideal spot, right next to the branch collar, without damaging the collar or leaving a stub. With anvil shears you have to leave a stub to avoid damaging the collar. (For more on branch collars and pruning, see *FG* #10 pp. 44-49.)

Bypass shears also do a better job than anvil shears of shearing through the relatively soft stems of herbaceous perennials and annuals. Anvil shears have a harder time cutting all the way through soft tissues. While some models of anvil shears, such as the Sandvik P38-20, performed better than I expected, most were no match for mushy hosta stems.

Anvil shears have one noteworthy advantage—their power to cut large, woody stems with ease. Few of the

Pruning shears anatomy

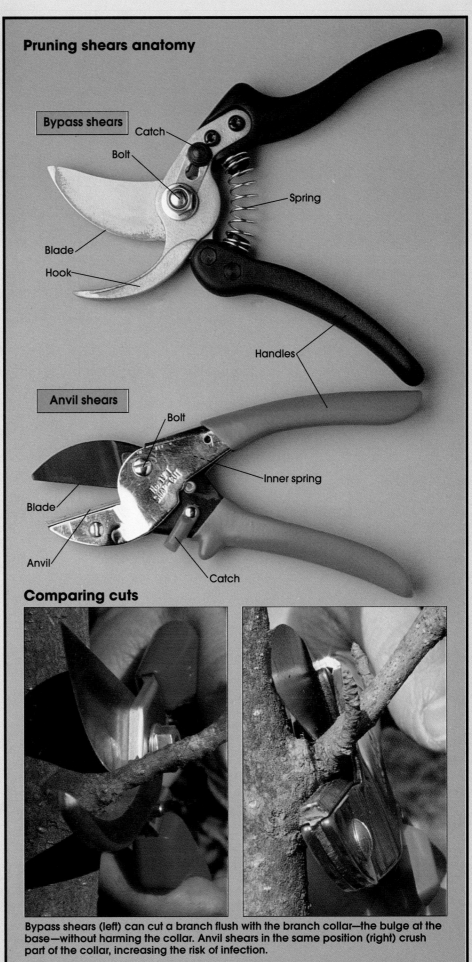

Bypass shears

Catch

Bolt

Spring

Blade

Hook

Handles

Anvil shears

Bolt

Inner spring

Blade

Anvil

Catch

Comparing cuts

Bypass shears (left) can cut a branch flush with the branch collar—the bulge at the base—without harming the collar. Anvil shears in the same position (right) crush part of the collar, increasing the risk of infection.

bypass shears I tried could slice through a branch larger than ½ in. in diameter without much effort; in many cases, I had to pause and adjust my grip to finish the job. The most powerful of the anvil shears, however, cut through branches as large as ¾ in. with little effort. (I am talking about live branches; dead wood is tougher.) I found the Rolcut 50, the Wallace P15T and P21H, and the Snap-Cut 19T to be particularly strong models.

Which class of shears is best for you depends on your needs. If you use shears primarily to make precise cuts on everything from flower stems to small branches, then bypass shears will serve you best. If, instead, you prune mostly woody stems and want shears that can cut larger branches with less effort, then anvil shears are for you. In the past I used bypass shears exclusively, but now that I've felt the power of a good anvil model, I've decided to have one of each.

Judging quality

Since basic designs are often similar, when you shop for pruning shears, focus on quality and comfort. You can

Photos: top, Susan Kahn; insets, Chris Curless

tell a lot about a pair of shears by holding it in your hand. Try the shears that your friends swear by, and take the tools on display at the hardware store or garden center out of their packages.

Shears should open and close smoothly, without resistance, but they should not be loose. Take one handle of an open pair of shears in each hand and push the handles back and forth against each other. If you detect a wobble, move on to the next model.

Bypass shears cut at the moving point where the edge of the blade passes the hook. You can get an idea of cutting performance by holding an open pair of shears up to a light and closing the handle slowly while you squint past the flat side of the blade. You should be able to see the contact point between blade and hook sweep from the back of the blade to the tip. If the blade makes poor contact with the hook, then the shears will tear the stem instead of cutting it.

The blade of anvil shears should make contact with the anvil all along its length. Where the blade fails to meet the anvil, the shears won't be able to cut all the way through the stem. To determine whether blade and anvil are making proper contact, hold a pair of closed shears up to the light. If you can see light peeking through, the shears will cut poorly.

Judging the quality of the materials in a pair of shears can be difficult, especially when it comes to the steel used to make the blade. Unless you're fairly knowledgeable about steel making, the claims on the packaging won't mean much to you. I learned that steel quality varies from manufacturer to manufacturer and from model to model. In general, more expensive shears have blades made of harder steel, which keeps a sharp edge longer. But even blades made of softer steel can perform well under average garden use. You just have to sharpen them more frequently.

Size and feel
Even the best made shears aren't worth much to you if they don't fit your hand comfortably. Women and men with small hands may find many shears too large, particularly the "professional" bypass shears. When the shears spring open, the lower handle can slip out of reach of the fingertips. In my relatively small hand, the Sandvik P1-22, with handles that stretch almost 7 in. across at the end, felt enormous. In

In a small hand, a pair of large bypass pruners, such as the one above, can swing open beyond the reach of the fingertips. The smaller pair shown below fits a small hand much more comfortably.

order to keep the shears in my grasp, I had to choke up on the handles. Men with large hands may have the opposite problem. There may not be room enough for their fingers on a pair of small shears such as the Village Blacksmith model 5040. Some manufacturers, such as Fiskars, offer the same model in two or even three sizes. But in most cases one size has to fit all, so it's important to try before you buy.

The comfort of the handles is also important. Many manufacturers say they've designed their handles "ergonomically," that is, they have designed the handles with the human hand in mind. The result is a great variety of handle shapes—some straight, others contoured with bumps and valleys. In general, I preferred shears with broad, gently curved handles. These handles spread the force you exert as you cut over a larger area, reducing the pressure on your palm and fingers to a minimum. By contrast, the shears with narrow handles or handles with relatively sharp curves tended to dig into my hand.

Left-handed gardeners unfortunately have few choices. Only Felco makes shears (models 9 and 10) especially designed for left-handed users. The catch, which locks shears closed when not in use, is located on the left side on most models, convenient only for right thumbs. Some shears, such as the Ames 23-187 and 23-188, have catches located on top of the upper handle, and a few models, including the True Friends 77, have catches in between the handles; these catches are easy to operate with either hand.

Anvil shears variations
On anvil shears, there are two design variations of note: pivoting anvils and ratchet blades. The Wallace P21H, the Rolcut 50, the Gardena 356 and the True Friends 77 have pivoting anvils. In the fully open position, the anvil is nearly parallel with the blade, which makes for a larger opening at the back of the jaws. As the jaws close, the anvil rotates slightly to meet the blade. I'm not sure if this design is superior; I'd like to hear the physics explained in layman's terms. One manufacturer's representative told me that the larger opening at the back of the jaws allows you to push a good-sized branch farther back into the jaws, where cutting leverage is greatest. Another representative told me that the purpose of the pivoting action is to roll the branch slightly during cutting in order

Photos: Chris Curless

to spread the force more evenly and thereby reduce the damage the anvil inflicts on the bark. I found that the Wallace and the Rolcut were indeed strong cutters, stronger than conventional anvil shears made by the same manufacturers, and that the damage they did to the bark was relatively slight. But they didn't outperform all of the anvil shears I examined.

Ratchet pruners, such as the Florian 701 and 901 and the Village Blacksmith 5033, let you cut a branch in several steps. With these models, if a branch is too large or hard for you to cut through it in one squeeze, you can relax your grip until a pin between the handles slips into the next notch in the rear of the blade. This gives you additional leverage so that you can squeeze again and make further progress in cutting the branch. Gardeners with weaker grips may find these shears very useful.

Repair

I hate to throw out a well-used pair of shears; to me they're like a pair of comfortable shoes. If you feel the same way, buy shears for which spare parts are available. The most expensive shears generally have the most replaceable parts; the least expensive shears often have blades and handles made from a single piece of steel and are held together with rivets, so they have no replaceable parts.

Since the spring tends to be the first thing to go on a pair of shears, check that you can buy a replacement. Volute springs, the ones that look like small, chrome croissants, have a longer life expectancy than other springs do, but all springs eventually break. When the spring in my shears broke, I found that the manufacturer no longer distributed that model. I still have the old pair; it's waiting rather forlornly for a suitable replacement spring.

Getting your money's worth

In general, with pruning shears, as with many other things, you get what you pay for. The most expensive models are assembled with replaceable parts made from costly materials. A pair of Sandvik P2-22 bypass shears, which has a dozen parts, all replaceable, represents the top of the line at a suggested retail price of $61.69. The least expensive shears have few or no replaceable parts and may cost one-tenth as much as high-end models. For example, a pair of Ames Eagle 23-103 bypass shears or 23-052 anvil

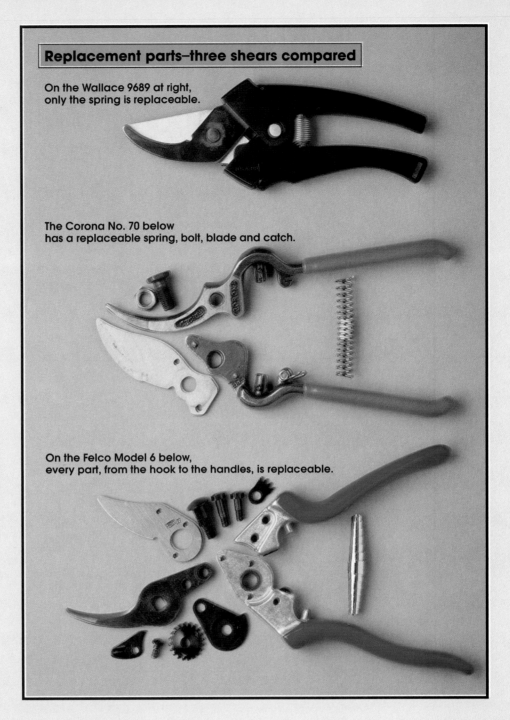

Replacement parts—three shears compared

On the Wallace 9689 at right, only the spring is replaceable.

The Corona No. 70 below has a replaceable spring, bolt, blade and catch.

On the Felco Model 6 below, every part, from the hook to the handles, is replaceable.

shears, available in a hardware or department store, has a suggested price of $5.90. Top-notch anvil shears cost less than their bypass counterparts. Among the models I looked at, only a few, including the True Friends 77 at $33.50, had suggested retail prices over $30. (Suggested retail prices are generally 20% to 100% higher than the prices in a store or a catalog.)

Pruning shears are available at hardware stores and garden centers, and by mail order. Some mail-order suppliers cater primarily to landscaping professionals and carry a wide selection of shears, including brands and models unfamiliar to most gardeners but worthy of consideration. (See Sources on p. 24.)

How much you spend depends on your pruning needs. If you use shears mostly to deadhead flowers, and you only occasionally prune trees and shrubs, an inexpensive pair may work fine for you and last indefinitely. If you do a lot of pruning on woody plants, then you'll probably want to spend a good deal more for shears that will perform well under heavy use and that can be repaired without much fuss if a part gives out. □

Chris Curless is an assistant editor at Fine Gardening.

Photo: Susan Kahn

Pruning Saws

The right tool makes cutting easier

by Ted Kipping

Pruning is sculpting with the life-force of plants. If you use the right tools, pruning a tree or shrub to keep it healthy and make it more beautiful can be one of the most enjoyable of gardening activities. Too often, however, gardeners are tempted to use whatever is handy. Yet a clean, sharp saw, one designed for pruning, not for carpentry work, can make the difference between an easy task that produces a smooth cut and a frustrating chore that produces a ragged cut, which is more conducive to disease.

A saw is the right tool for pruning branches that are too big to cut with shears or loppers. (For a review of shears, see "Pruning Shears" on pp. 22-25.) There are so many choices in saws that the average gardener perusing a catalogue or entering a well-stocked tool section of a garden center or hardware store might well be confused. I've been pruning trees professionally for 25 years and have run my own business for 17. In the course of my work, I've tried just about every saw available, and I can tell you from experience, a good saw makes pruning a lot easier (see Sources on p. 28).

Many designs available

Saws vary widely in design. The blades range from just 6 in. to 24 in. long (and longer on saws intended for heavy-duty work). Some blades are curved, some straight. The number of saw teeth per inch, the way the teeth are arranged and the way they cut also vary. You'll find a choice of handle styles, too. On a few, the

A coarse blade, with 4½ teeth per inch, which cuts on the pull stroke and is best suited for cutting up big logs; not for fine pruning

A bow-saw blade, which cuts on the push stroke

A Swedish blade, with 7 teeth per inch, which cuts on the push and the pull strokes

A Japanese-style anti-friction blade, which cuts on the pull stroke

Pruning saw blades vary in size and style.

blade folds into the handle to protect it when you're not working.

Different saws are designed for specific jobs. Nobody has made the perfect all-purpose pruning saw yet, so you have to choose depending on the size of the limb you're cutting, its placement on the tree or shrub, and the length of time you're pruning. If

you're working only an hour or two at a time, the blade is the most important consideration. If you're pruning all day long, consider the handle first, then get the best blade you can on a handle with a comfortable grip.

Blade choices

The number of saw teeth per inch affects the cut. A blade can have up to ten teeth per inch, but seven or eight teeth per inch is a good choice for the home owner who is pruning trees and shrubs. (Sometimes you'll see teeth referred to as points.) A coarse four teeth per inch is usually found on large saws and is best for cutting big logs in half, not for fine landscape pruning.

You may also see the word "kerf" used to describe saw teeth. Kerf refers to the way the teeth are out slightly from the vertical. You can see the kerf if you hold the blade perpendicular to a flat surface, teeth-side-up. The angle reduces friction and pinching on the blade by making the cutting surface wider than the top of the blade. Some designers also apply Teflon coatings to the blades to reduce friction, a great help until it wears off, which is fairly rapidly. American saws tend to have a pronounced kerf. The newest style of blades, first produced by the Japanese, has no kerf; friction is reduced on these saws because the blades have been ground to make the top narrower than the cutting surface.

The combination of teeth per inch plus kerf results in characteristic cuts. Fewer teeth per inch and a pronounced kerf make for a coarse scoring pattern on the cut surface and may leave a zigzag edge on the bark. More teeth per inch and a small kerf make a smoother cut. A clean, smooth cut promotes formation of wound wood, which

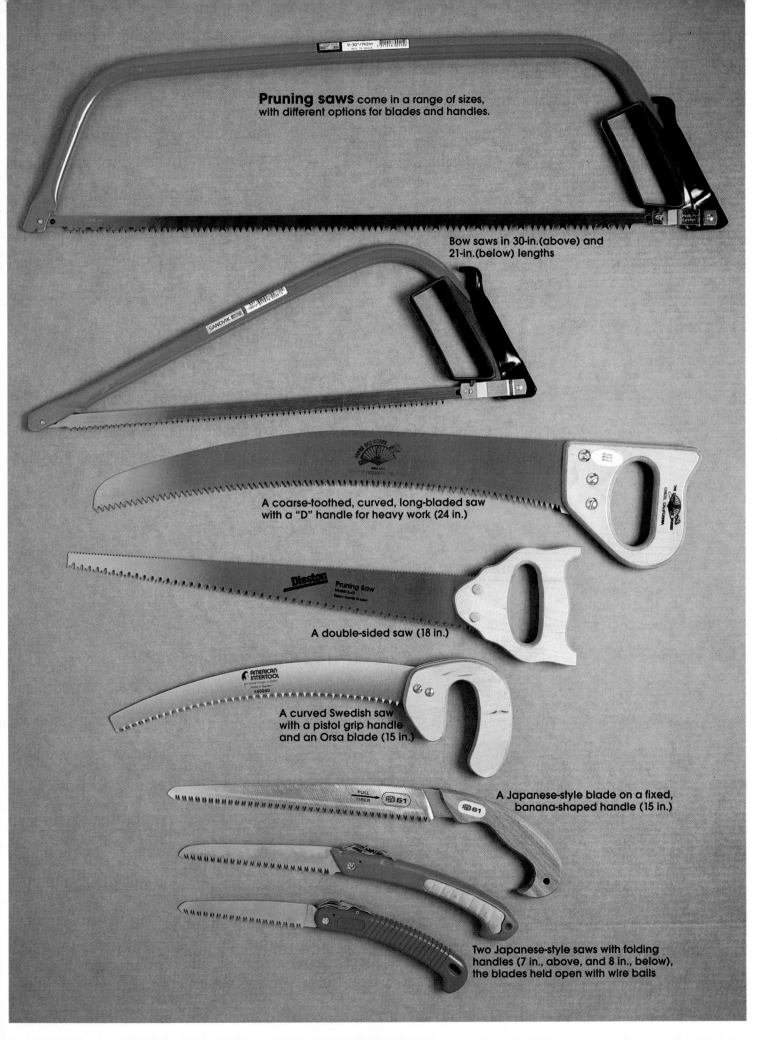

Pruning saws come in a range of sizes, with different options for blades and handles.

Bow saws in 30-in.(above) and 21-in.(below) lengths

A coarse-toothed, curved, long-bladed saw with a "D" handle for heavy work (24 in.)

A double-sided saw (18 in.)

A curved Swedish saw with a pistol grip handle and an Orsa blade (15 in.)

A Japanese-style blade on a fixed, banana-shaped handle (15 in.)

Two Japanese-style saws with folding handles (7 in., above, and 8 in., below), the blades held open with wire bails protects a cut surface more readily than a ragged one does. (For more information on pruning techniques, see *Fine Gardening* #10, pp. 44-49.)

Blades can cut on the pull stroke, the push stroke, or both. If you prune mostly in your own garden and not as a job, it probably won't make any difference which type of blade you select, because the pruning saws will work in all situations, albeit more efficiently in some than in others. The following information, however, will help you understand the differences and guide you in your choices.

A straight blade usually cuts on the push stroke, like an American carpentry saw, and uses your body weight to add stability to the blade when you are cutting something lower than your waist. A curved blade usually cuts on the pull stroke and uses your body weight to stabilize your cutting hand when you are cutting something at your chest height or higher. The majority of pruning saws currently available cut only on the pull stroke. On a really long blade, the curve helps a little bit by positioning the far end of the blade down into the wood for you. A few blades cut on both the push and the pull, which utilizes all your effort efficiently, making the job go faster.

Handle choices

Handles come in four styles—bow handle, "D" handle, pistol grip and banana handle. A bow saw looks more or less like a bow for archery, and its handle is a metal tube that curves from one end of the blade to the other. The "D" handle, shaped like that letter, looks like the handle of a carpenter's saw and gives the most hand protection. Pistol grip handles are similar to "D" handles, but are open at the bottom. "D" and pistol handles fit the natural grip of the hand very comfortably, whether you're cutting from top down or making an undercut (a cut made upward from the underside of a branch). The newest design is the banana handle, which is curved like the fruit. Although the banana handle works fine for most cuts, it is tiring to use for undercuts, because your wrist is twisted while you're pulling upward. It's fine for occasional use, but as a professional, I wouldn't want to use one

for undercuts all day long. Occasionally a handle is padded, but you should be wearing gloves whenever you use pruning tools, so the padding is not absolutely necessary.

Saws with handles that don't fold up are better stored in a scabbard (sheath) worn at the belt, while those with folding handles can be carried around in a deep pocket. I think one company, Felco, offers an example of a well-thought-out folding saw. The banana-shaped handle is bright red, so if you absent-mindedly set it down, you can find it again. It's also ridged, so you can hold on to it, even if your

For cutting upward from the underside of a branch, a pistol grip handle (above) puts less strain on the wrist than a banana-shaped handle (below).

SOURCES

The author recommends the following mail-order suppliers, which sell the saws described in this article and many more, as well as other professional-quality tools.

American Arborist Supplies, 862 South Matlack St., West Chester, PA 19382, 800-441-8381. Catalog free.

The Bishop Co., P.O. Box 870, Whittier, CA 90608, 800-421-4833. Catalog free.

A.M. Leonard, Inc., P.O. Box 816, Piqua, OH 45356, 513-773-2694. Catalog free.

gloves get slimy, and it has a secure locking wire bail, or clasp. A branch of 3 in. in diameter is probably the largest it can cut.

I really like the bright red handle. Plain wooden handles and the spiffy black plastic ones tend to disappear into the landscape if you put them down. (I've also had saws fall out of a scabbard when I was at the top of a tree, and a wood handle is just about impossible to find when a big tree swallows it.) If you buy a wood or black handle, I suggest making it more visible by sticking on a swatch of bright tape or applying one of those brightly colored vinyl dips sold in hardware stores to recoat tool handles.

If you choose a folding saw, be sure to select one that locks the blade in place securely in the open position during use, to prevent a painful accident. The best lock is a wire bail. Some saws have wing nuts as locks, but nuts aren't as reliable. If you tighten the nut securely enough to keep the blade from folding, you won't be able to loosen it by hand. The nut also tends to bang into the bark or into your hand.

Saw choices

Bow saws—Probably the most saw for the money is the bow saw. The blade is a thin ribbon of hardened steel with deeply notched and very sharp teeth. The teeth are often arranged in sets with a "gullet" in between (an open space that allows debris to clear out), which reduces friction. The thinness of the blade also reduces friction, making the cut fast and clean. Bow saws cut on the push stroke.

With a bow saw, you can do almost anything you can with a chain saw, but quietly. It's great for making quick work of limbs thicker than 3 in. for or reducing a pile of logs to firewood. Because of the width of the bow, however, it's suited to removing only a branch with lots of room between it and other limbs. I'd use a bow saw to remove thick, widely spaced branches or to cut up a tree that fell across the driveway—it's not for pruning inside your camellia.

A good bow saw costs from $8 to $15, half the price of a big, professional, hand-pruning saw. A bow saw will do the same jobs a big saw will, but with a lot less work, because the thin blade creates so little friction. They are so inexpensive that I think they are a good choice to have in your tool collection if you ever face any chores like cutting up firewood or removing storm debris.

Bow saws come in many sizes. Some are so big they require two people to use them (they're used for cutting up trees, not for hand-pruning), while others are as small as 21 in. long. I'd recommend finding a bow saw that feels comfortable in your hand. Store it indoors and try to remember to keep the protective strip that covers the blade when you buy it. It looks like packaging, and most people throw it away, but it will protect both the blade and your hands when you are rummaging around near it in the garage or toolshed.

Medium-size saws—Saws with narrow, short blades (about 12 in. to 15 in. long), are the most useful ones for gardeners who are pruning shrubs and small trees, not huge limbs. They are better for working in tight spots than big saws with wide, long blades are. The tip is likely to be a lot narrower than the handle end, so you can maneuver in close to your work. Most of the medium-size saws cut on the pull stroke, which will be especially advantageous for cutting branches chest-high or above. You can find them with "D," pistol-grip or banana handles.

There is a blade of Swedish design, Orsa, which cuts in both directions. Its long teeth are much finer than those on American-style blades, with a smaller kerf, yielding a better-quality final cut. Despite the fine teeth, the Orsa blade cuts quickly because there is no wasted arm motion. Mail-order suppliers don't necessarily indicate the brand of blade on their saws; however, I do know that A.M. Leonard uses an Orsa blade on its Swedish pruning saw.

Big saws—When you're looking for saws, you might also see large, long-bladed saws about the size of carpenters' saws (about 20 in. to 24 in. long), with wide, blunt ends and coarse teeth. Because the end of the saw is wide, it's hard to maneuver it into tight spaces. These saws are not very useful for pruning trees.

Large, long-bladed saws are usually designed to cut either on the push or the pull part of the stroke. They re-

quire a great deal of strength to start a cut. To continue cutting, they also require that you fully extend your arm, even though this position does not allow you to use your full strength. You often have to use your free hand to guide the blade—it's important to wear sturdy gloves. Long-bladed saws tend to make a very coarse cut. However, these saws do have terrifically comfortable "D" handles.

A few long-bladed saws have cutting teeth on the top and bottom edges of the blade. One set of teeth is coarse, the other fine. The "D" handle can be grasped in either direction. It's difficult to use such a saw without the top of the blade inadvertently slicing into a nearby branch that you didn't want to remove. Having teeth on both edges increases friction on deep cuts, too.

Several manufacturers produce pruning saws that fold into their handles for storing. A wire bail secures the blade in the open position for working.

Blades on the cutting edge

The most impressive breakthrough to appear in our market is the saws inspired by Japanese carpentry tools. The blades, which have no kerf, are thin, razor sharp, clean-cutting and *fast*. American and European companies now use these blades, too, and you might see them described as "turbo" or "frictionless" rather than as Japanese blades.

These saws are so sharp that you must wear a glove even on the hand that's not holding the saw. (Even with 25 years of experience, I cut myself badly the first time I worked with one. Other tree trimmers have reported the same unexpected experience.) Although these saws cut only on the pull stroke, the better ones are so fast they still outcut anything else around, and the surface of the cut looks as if you had finished it with sandpaper.

Some of these Japanese blades are too thin to tackle branches much thicker than 2 in. in diameter without breaking. Blade breakage was a common problem in the first wave of imports. Now you can find the same tooth design on blades of greater substance.

More useful are blades that are thicker at the teeth and thinner at the top. The thicker blades twist less and are reinforced at the base, which dampens the vibrations caused by enthusiastic sawing much the way putting your thumb on a cymbal will silence it. Learn to slow down as you near the end of a cut, too, because it causes less vibration and reduces chances of bark ripping. Most of these newer saw blades come with a banana-shaped handle, either fixed or hinged with a locking arrangement.

My ideal pruning saw doesn't exist yet. It would probably use the best of the new breed of blades, but be designed to cut in both directions, and be supported by a comfortable "D" or pistol grip handle of a permanent bright color.

Keep your tools clean and sharp, pay close attention to each cut (a sort of meditative Zen approach can ensue) and enjoy the process. □

Ted Kipping is a certified arborist with the International Society of Arboriculture. He has been pruning trees in San Francisco, California, for 25 years.

Garden Hoses

How to choose the kind you need

An opaque garden hose coils with
a neighbor that shows mesh reinforcing
below its clear covering. You can't judge a hose
by its cover. Suppleness and durability depend on construction.

by Mark Kane

Visit any garden center in spring
and you're sure to smell plastic and
see coils of new hoses. The packaging might say "Good," "Better" and
"Best." It might claim extra plies, great
suppleness or a mix of rubber and
vinyl. And prices will vary widely,
from $5 a coil to $20 and more. How
can you pick the hose you need? What
are the differences between garden
hoses? For answers, I talked to hose
manufacturers and engineers, and
looked at the garden hoses on the
market. Here's what I found.

Hose design

Hose design is tricky. A hose has to turn
around corners and bend into coils
yet withstand the same water pressure
as the pipes in your house—at least
40 psi (pounds per square inch) and
in some cities, 90 psi.

Imagine a 1-in. cube with a 90-lb.
sack of cement perched on top. Now
place the cube on a sheet of rubber
stretched taut in mid-air. The pressure
on the rubber is 90 psi. Roll the rubber
into a tube and you have a hose,
which must resist the same 90 psi at
every point without stretching and
still remain flexible.

To understand how hose makers
balance suppleness and strength,
you have to look at hose construction.
The walls of a hose consist of two or
three layers called plies. The cheapest
hoses have only two plies: an inner
tube and a covering. Higher quality
hoses add a ply of synthetic yarn
around the inner tube to resist bursting. The yarn ply is generally in
two parts, a spiral winding and a
sheath of mesh (see the cutaway on
the facing page).

You also have to know a few things
about the plastics in hose coverings

and inner tubes. Most hoses are made
of polyvinyl chloride (PVC), a clear,
colorless plastic. (It's still PVC when the
packaging on a hose says "vinyl.") To
alter PVC, hose makers add various
plasticizers for flexibility, fillers for
resistance to abrasion and sunlight,
and colorants. In higher-quality hoses,
synthetic rubber is mixed with the
PVC to improve flexibility and resistance to abrasion.

Suppleness comes at a price. The
PVC of the inner tube has to be
elastic, which limits its strength. To
keep the inner tube from bursting, the
yarn ply must be wound and knit
closely, which takes extra yarn. The
covering must have enough thickness
and strength to aid the yarn ply and
still be flexible. As you might expect,
flexible PVC and a strong yarn ply
raise the cost of the hose. The cheapest
hoses have no reinforcing, so they must
be made of stiff plastic for strength,
so they kink easily and are hard to
maneuver and coil.

How to shop for a hose

What are the signs of hose quality? The first is price. Provided the retailer is playing fair, higher-priced hoses are more flexible and long-lived than less expensive hoses. Warranties tend to parallel prices and range from five years to lifetime.

Couplings are also a sign of quality. The least expensive are relatively thin brass (see photo at right). The swivel on the female end is round, with ridges to improve your grip. (Some round swivels are sheathed with a thick, soft plastic ring to make tightening easier—they're helpful if you find it difficult or painful to tighten round swivels.) The sturdiest and most expensive couplings are thicker, and the swivel has flat facets that allow you to grip it tightly or tighten it with a wrench. The tang—the brass tube that goes inside the hose—generally holds the hose more strongly on heavy couplings than on thinner couplings.

Flexibility is another indication of quality. It can be hard to gauge in the store, since hoses are generally sold in coils bound with several twist-ties. I suggest you ask if you can undo one tie and test 18 in. of hose end. Bend the hose in a U-shape and slowly bring the two legs of the "U" together. A high quality hose bends with little force and makes a tight curve without kinking. A cheap hose takes more force to bend and kinks readily at the center of a tight curve.

The number of plies is a less certain mark of quality. For one thing, hose makers differ in the way they count plies—some count spiral wrap and mesh as two plies, some as one ply. For another thing, some plies have little effect on performance—for example, a film of plastic on the outside for color or a film between the inner tube and the covering that helps bind them together. I have two suggestions: test flexibility and don't pay a premium price just because the maker says a hose has five or six plies.

How do you pick the hose you need? Ask yourself how you use garden hoses and how much you want to pay. If you use a garden hose regularly under tough conditions, dragging a long length across the driveway and around trees and buildings, pay more and buy a high-quality hose. If you rarely use a hose, don't have to pull it far and don't mind a little wrestling, buy a less expensive hose.

There's one other thing to consider when buying a hose—its capacity. If you water by hand and your reach is no more than 75 ft., a ½-in. diameter hose will do. If you use a good-sized sprinkler or run water more than 75 ft., buy a ⅝-in. diameter hose.

Hose care

Garden hoses last longer with good care. Avoid kinking them, keep them out of the sun when they're not in use, carry and pull them gently, and store them indoors over the winter if you live in a cold climate.

Sunlight attacks garden hoses. It breaks down the plastic covering, making it first weak and then brittle. Eventually the covering cracks and then only the inner tube and the yarn ply (if there is one) contain the water pressure. When you're not using the hose, coil it loosely and store it in shade. If your spigot is in the sun, shelter the hose or disconnect it and move it to the shade.

Handle a hose gently. Pulling it hard can strain the couplings and the tube. If you stretch a hose from a spigot, the inner tube can bend against the edge of the tang and tear. If the hose is hot (from being in the sun), the plastic is stretchier than usual and may pull off the tang.

When you store a hose in the off-season, observe a few rules. Drain the water. Coil the hose loosely or wind it on hose reel. Finally, store it indoors, away from solvents, oil and other chemicals that could harm the plastic.

How long does a hose last? If you use a cheap hose hard, leaving it out in the sun continuously, it may crack open after a few years. At the other extreme, if you treat a top-quality hose with care, it can last ten years and more. The high first cost turns into a long-term bargain. ∎

Mark Kane is executive editor of Fine Gardening. *He uses 100 ft. of hose to garden on near-sand in Waterbury, Connecticut.*

The couplings on the left are made of thinner brass and indicate a lower-quality hose; the heavier couplings on the right indicate a higher-quality hose. The octagonal shape of the heavy swivel gives a better grip for hand or wrench.

A cutaway in a garden hose reveals three plies—a green covering, a black inner tube, and reinforcing, which combines a spiral of yarn and a mesh sheath. One sign of better quality hoses, reinforcing allows the use of more flexible plastic.

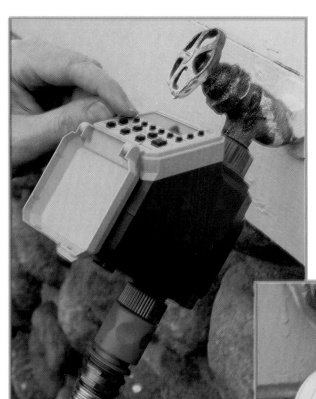

Timers for Watering the Garden

Two gadgets mind the hose when you can't

By programming an electronic timer (above) or setting the dial on a mechanical timer (right), you can water your garden while you do other things.

by Sven Hanson

If hand-watering or tending a hose and sprinkler takes more time than you can spare, a water timer will help. A water timer is a valve in a box that has two hose fittings. You attach one fitting to a spigot and then thread your hose onto the other fitting. When you turn the dial or punch a few buttons, the timer will automatically measure out water as you prune roses, sleep, or run errands.

I decided to look into water timers when I found myself sneaking out of work to run home and turn off my drip-irrigation system. (A mud bog would be an exceedingly expensive garden feature here in Albuquerque, New Mexico.) I went to a nearby home-supplies store and found a whole wall of timing gizmos. Some were mechanical, driven by the flow of water or an internal spring. Some

were electronic—little battery-powered computers, actually. By pushing buttons, you can set up as many as eight separate watering programs on these electronic models.

I wasn't sure which timer was right for me, so I tried several. Here's what I learned.

Mechanical timers

Mechanical water timers resemble kitchen timers. You turn a calibrated dial to get water, selecting the number of gallons you want delivered. These timers work like water meters, measuring the volume of water that passes through them. The water drives a turbine, which turns gears that rotate the dial back to zero. Then, instead of ringing a bell, the timer turns off the water. (One mechanical water timer is an exception: the Gardena 1185 measures time, not water volume.)

If you've been watering by the clock, you'll have to practice with a mechanical timer for a while before you get a feel for the relationship between gallons and time. Mechanical

timers deliver precise quantities of water, but the delivery time varies according to the rate at which water flows through the timer. Your water pressure and the sprinklers, bubblers or drip irrigation emitters you attach to the hose all affect how long it takes to deliver a specific quantity of water.

Mechanical water timers are reliable, easy to use and inexpensive—they sell for as little as $10. They're perfect for those occasions when you want to run a sprinkler or a soaker hose for an hour or two but you won't be there to turn it off.

Mechanical timers have one big limitation—although they turn water off, they can't turn it on automatically. You must turn the dial to get water, so a mechanical timer can't water while you're at work or on vacation unless you have a friend or a neighborhood teenager come by and start it.

Electronic timers

Electronic water timers combine a clock, an electric water valve and a small computer that opens and closes the valve at the times you set. The computer has a memory that is kept alive by batteries; it always remembers to both start and stop the flow of water, allowing you to forget about watering almost entirely.

Electronic timers can be amazingly versatile. The most sophisticated models can water up to eight different times on selected watering days—great for establishing new plantings. Also, many models have long maximum run times—12 hours or more. (Mechanical timers have a maximum of about four hours to six hours.) A couple of models have a misting feature that greenhouse owners and gardeners starting new lawns would appreciate: they turn the water on for just a few seconds or a few minutes several times an hour. Finally, all electronic timers allow you to turn the water on and off manually without erasing the program.

Power has its price. Electronic timers sell for anywhere from $30 to $70, depending on the features they offer.

They also can be tricky to program (more difficult than a microwave oven, easier than a VCR). You must follow several steps—entering watering days, starting times and durations—in strict order. A label inside the hinged cover on most models gives a short course in programming, but you'll still need the manual to chart more intricate programs or to solve problems.

Electronic timers have another drawback: they don't know to pause when it rains. Here in the desert Southwest, it's hard to overwater most plants, but where rainfall is more plentiful, an automatic watering regime can be downright dangerous. If you forget to change your timer's program, you can literally drown your plants. To address this problem, one manufacturer, Rainmatic (now sold under the Nelson name), makes a moisture-sensing soil probe as an accessory to its timers. The probe prevents the timer from watering when the soil is moist, then allows the watering regimen to

resume when the soil dries. Forgetful gardeners may want to spend the additional $30 for this convenience.

How to choose

The timers I tried functioned as the manufacturers promised, so the choice depends on your watering needs. If dry spells are infrequent in your area, you can save money, batteries and the headache of programming by buying an inexpensive mechanical model. Where drought is a way of life, I recommend paying more for the hands-off convenience of an electronic timer.

Whatever you choose, don't worry about finding yourself with too much extra time on your hands. No machine can deadhead flowers or pick apricots properly. You'll still have plenty of hands-on gardening to enjoy. □

Sven Hanson is a gardener, a woodworker and a former engineering student. He lives in Albuquerque, New Mexico.

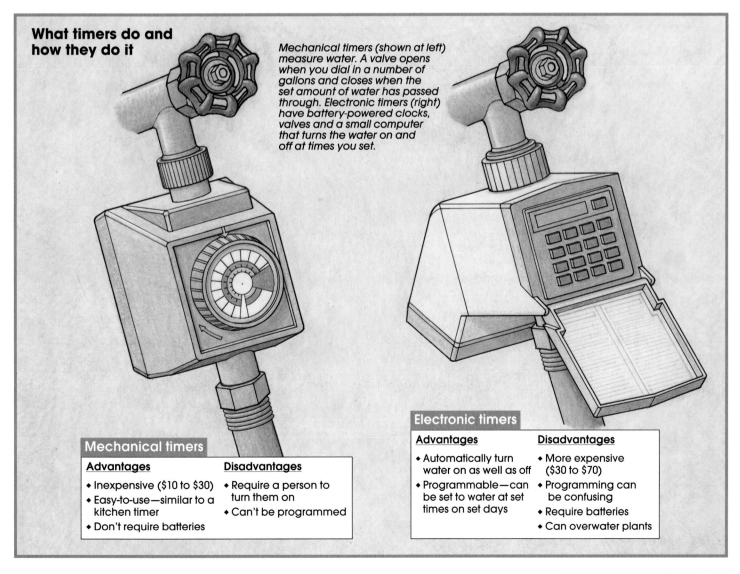

What timers do and how they do it

Mechanical timers (shown at left) measure water. A valve opens when you dial in a number of gallons and closes when the set amount of water has passed through. Electronic timers (right) have battery-powered clocks, valves and a small computer that turns the water on and off at times you set.

Mechanical timers

Advantages
- Inexpensive ($10 to $30)
- Easy-to-use—similar to a kitchen timer
- Don't require batteries

Disadvantages
- Require a person to turn them on
- Can't be programmed

Electronic timers

Advantages
- Automatically turn water on as well as off
- Programmable—can be set to water at set times on set days

Disadvantages
- More expensive ($30 to $70)
- Programming can be confusing
- Require batteries
- Can overwater plants

Glistening with sunlight, the stream from a pump sprayer reaches up into the branches of a small tree. For gardeners who frequently need to spray one-half gallon or more, pump sprayers offer versatility and economy.

Pump Sprayers

How to choose the right model for your needs

by Chris Curless

Most gardeners need a pump sprayer at one time or another. They may have to fight off a horde of hungry Japanese beetles with an insecticide or control a nasty outbreak of powdery mildew with a fungicide. They may want to clear out a large patch of tenacious perennial weeds with herbicides. Or they may just need to perk up some yellowing plants with a good dose of liquid seaweed.

If you frequently need to spray more than a few ounces of garden chemicals, consider buying a pump sprayer. A pump sprayer has a portable tank with a pump, a hose, a wand and a valve to control delivery of the spray. You pressurize the tank with a few strokes of the pump. Then, with the tank in one hand and the valve in the other, you can handily spray big gardens or big plants.

Pump sprayers can save money as well as time. For jobs requiring a half-gallon or more of spray, mixing your own is more economical than buying pre-mixed sprays in aerosol cans or bottles with finger pumps. When you use a pump sprayer, you mix a concentrated liquid with water, and the result, spray for spray, is much less expensive than pre-mixed chemicals. For example, at a nearby garden center, I priced a 24-oz. spray bottle of Roundup herbicide at $5.00, or 20 cents per ounce. A pint of Roundup concentrate costs more than twice as much—$12.00—but makes about 5 gal. (640 oz.) of spray mix. So, at just two cents an ounce, spray mixed from concentrate costs one-tenth as much as ready-to-use spray.

Pump sprayers have other advantages. They have adjustable nozzles that deliver a range of sprays, from a fine mist that can thoroughly wet a tangle of leaves and stems to a thin jet that can reach to the tops of 25-ft. to 30-ft. trees. Pump sprayers also have wands that extend the reach of your arm, allowing you to spray the ground without stooping or to reach inside a shrub to coat the undersides of the leaves.

You may find yourself overwhelmed by the variety of sprayers available. There are over 100 different models marketed for home use, and every garden center, hardware store and mail-order catalog offers a different selection—from one model to as many as a half dozen or more. To make sense of the choices, I called major manufacturers of pump sprayers and asked for samples in the most common sizes—1-gal. to 3-gal. I examined 23 sprayers and tried them in my yard. Here's what I learned.

How pump sprayers work

Most 1-gal. to 3-gal. sprayers operate on the principle that air can be compressed and liquids can't. The sprayers have a maximum fill line, at about three-quarters of the tank's capacity. When you pump the sprayer, you force air under pressure into the space above the liquid. The more you pump, the higher the pressure becomes. Then, when you open the valve, the compressed air forces the liquid up a plastic supply tube, through the hose and out the nozzle (see drawing at right).

You usually have to pump a sprayer several times to empty the tank. As the amount of liquid in the sprayer drops, so does the pressure. Eventually the sprayer fizzles instead of spraying, and then you have to pump it again.

Because of the need for air space, there is usually a difference between the nominal capacity of the tank and the liquid capacity. Most manufacturers classify their 2-gal. and 3-gal. sprayers by the nominal capacity. So a 3-gal. sprayer usually has a working capacity of only 2½ gal.; and a 2-gal. sprayer typically holds 1½ gal. If you want two gallons of spray mix, you must either use a 3-gal. sprayer or fill a smaller sprayer twice. To make the situation even more confusing, 1-gal. sprayers are exceptions—they really do have room for 1 gal. of liquid. When you compare sprayers, be sure to learn how much they hold. Read the fine print on the box or take a look at the tank itself.

One kind of sprayer operates without compressed air. It's called a trombone—or slide—sprayer. You hold it with both hands and pump a sliding part back and forth. The pump draws liquid through a hose placed in an open bucket or attached to a non-pressurized tank. Trombone sprayers spray only when you pump, so they require continuous effort, which can be taxing when the adjustable nozzle is tightened to create a mist spray. But their most serious drawback is the risk of knocking over the bucket of spray while you are working.

Construction and maintenance

The differences between sprayers lie in their construction, comfort and convenience (see photo on p. 37). For materials, the ideal choices are basically plastic or metal. Tanks are made of polyethylene plastic, stainless steel or galvanized steel; galvanized steel tanks are usually coated with a thin layer of epoxy. All three materials are durable (stainless steel is virtually indestructible). But finding a metal sprayer may not be easy; most sprayers in hardware stores and garden centers have plastic tanks. Plastic has merit—it's lightweight and corrosion-resistant. Many plastic tanks are also translucent, so you can see the liquid in the tank.

Sprayer hoses are made from a variety of materials. Some are vinyl-like plastic; they have a cheap feel and tend to be very stiff. The hose of the Smith PNN6, for example, fought me as I used it, toppling a full tank when I had it sitting on the ground. Other hoses are more flexible, with a rubbery feel, and some are reinforced by nylon braiding, which allows them to be supple, yet strong.

The materials in the wand and nozzle also vary. Top-of-the-line sprayers tend to have wands and nozzles made of brass, which is durable and resists corrosion. But the alternative—plastic—has similar virtues. I like the weight of brass, but plastic is more flexible. I accidentally stepped on one brass wand and bent it enough that I had to order a replacement; a plastic wand would probably have survived.

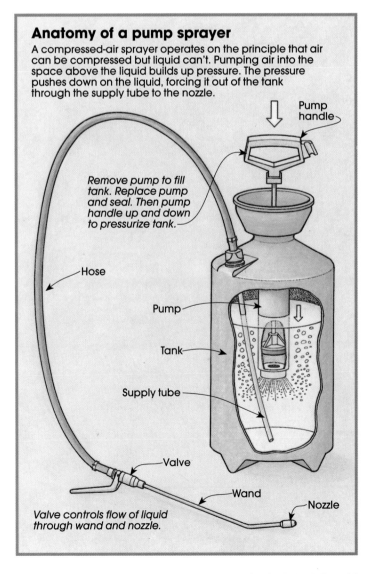

Anatomy of a pump sprayer

A compressed-air sprayer operates on the principle that air can be compressed but liquid can't. Pumping air into the space above the liquid builds up pressure. The pressure pushes down on the liquid, forcing it out of the tank through the supply tube to the nozzle.

Remove pump to fill tank. Replace pump and seal. Then pump handle up and down to pressurize tank.

Pump handle

Hose

Pump

Tank

Supply tube

Valve

Wand

Nozzle

Valve controls flow of liquid through wand and nozzle.

Illustration: Vince Babak

A cone of mist from a sprayer nozzle covers the needles and small branches of a pine tree. Adjustable nozzles allow you to vary spray from a strong stream to a fine mist.

Using a sprayer safely

Garden chemicals are dangerous. Handling them improperly can result in injury to you, to bystanders or to the environment. Here are a few guidelines for safe spraying. Read the sprayer manual and product labels for additional safety instructions.

- **Spray the proper chemical.** Before you spray a pest, identify it. It is unwise and illegal to use a chemical not listed for the pest you want to control.

- **Choose the time you spray with care.** Avoid spraying when wind will cause spray to drift. To prevent run-off, don't spray when rain threatens. Also, avoid the heat of the day; chemicals sprayed in warm weather can burn plants. The best time to spray is usually in the early morning or evening.

- **Wear appropriate clothing.** Boots, long pants, a long-sleeved shirt and rubber gloves are minimum standard equipment. The chemical's label may also direct you to wear a wide-brimmed hat and goggles.

- **Test your sprayer before you use it.** Give your sprayer a trial run with plain water. You don't want to discover a pump or hose leak when the tank is full of mixed chemicals.

- **Mix only as much as you need.** If you err, err by mixing less. To get rid of excess mix, you have to spray it on another target, or you have to pour it into a container for disposal as directed by your state environmental protection agency.

- **Follow proper clean-up procedures.** After spraying, wash your sprayer both inside and out with clean water, and spray rinse water on the targets you sprayed before. Store the sprayer upside down with the pump removed to allow the tank to dry out. The final step is to wash your clothes and your body. Launder clothes worn while spraying separately from other clothing.   —C.C.

No matter what a sprayer is made of, the key to longevity is proper maintenance. Sprayers need thorough cleaning after every use. Garden chemicals—even in trace amounts—quickly corrode metal and plastic parts if not washed away. Cleaning is critical if you spray herbicides. If you leave any herbicide residues in the tank, the next time you spray a chemical other than herbicides, you run the risk of injuring valuable plants. Rather than take chances, gardeners who use herbicides often buy a second sprayer for herbicides only. (For more on cleaning, see "Using a sprayer safely" below left.)

When a sprayer part fails, you need to replace it. Most manufacturers include information on ordering spare parts in the manual. Gaskets and O-rings, the small rubber parts that prevent leaks, tend to dry out and fail more often than other sprayer parts, so many manufacturers offer gasket and O-ring replacement kits through stores.

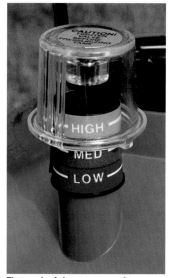

The colorful pressure-release valve on top of this sprayer tank serves three purposes: it shows the relative pressure inside the tank; it depressurizes the tank when you pull up on the clear plastic cup; and it vents excess pressure.

Comfort and convenience

All of the sprayers I tried—from the least expensive, no-frills models to the top of the line—did the basic job. They differed widely, however, in their comfort and convenience.

The most onerous part of using a sprayer is carrying it around. Water is heavy; a gallon weighs 8.3 lbs., so a sprayer that holds 2½ gal. weighs over 20 lbs. when it's full. Lugging that weight around becomes tiring quite quickly. Three-gal. sprayers usually come with a webbed, nylon shoulder strap. The strap keeps your arm from getting tired, but it soon cuts into your shoulder. If you don't often need to spray more than a gallon at a time, I would recommend you buy a smaller sprayer; you can always mix extra batches if you need to spray a little more.

One of the chief benefits of using a pump sprayer is that it allows you to apply garden chemicals exactly where you want them. Because the tank is usually either in your hand, on the ground or on your shoulder, you need a hose long enough to allow you to extend your arm. If the hose is short, you may have to hold the tank in an uncomfortable position to increase your reach (see photo on p. 34). Of the sprayers I examined, the hoses on the Spray Doc 101P and the Hudson 60071, at 30 in. and 31½ in. respectively, were too short for me. I preferred the longer hoses of the Smith PNN6 (48 in.) and the Solo 456 (55 in.).

The length of the wand also determines how well you will be able to deliver the spray where you want it. Standard wands on the models I looked at varied in length from just 9 in. on the Hudson 60071 to 22 in. on the Smith Max-11 and the Solo 456. Two models, the Tecnoma T200 Pro and the Suncast GT 300, have wands that telescope from 21 in. to 37 in. in length. The extra reach can come in handy.

Photos: left, Mark Kane; right, Chris Curless

The choices in pump sprayers

Telescoping wand extends reach.

Plastic wand and nozzle

1-gal. tank

3-gal. tank

Graphite Tank Sprayer

2-gal. tank

Stainless steel tank

hudson Leader Sprayer

Solo 456

CHAPIN Premier

Brass wand and nozzle

Epoxy-coated, galvanized-steel tank

Polyethylene plastic tanks

Model 1000P

Pressure-release valve

Trombone sprayer

When you shop for a pump sprayer, you'll find a range of choices in construction and in tank sizes. Many models offer comfort and convenience features, including shoulder straps, pressure-release valves and telescoping wands. You may also run across a trombone sprayer, which requires continuous back and forth pumping to deliver the spray.

Most sprayers come with adjustable nozzles. Adjustable nozzles allow you to vary the spray from a mist to a jet by rotating the tip. Some manufacturers also offer specialty nozzles. The Suncast GT 300, the Chapin 1243 and the Smith Max-11 come with a fan nozzle that emits spray in a broad, narrow band; this nozzle is probably most useful for spraying rows of vegetables. The Tecnoma T200 Pro comes with a combination fan nozzle and spray shield that screws to the end of the wand. The spray shield limits drift, preventing chemicals from landing away from the target—particularly important with herbicides. Other manufacturers offer similar equipment, but it's optional.

When you are finished spraying, you must release the pressure from the tank before cleaning and storing the sprayer. With some models, this procedure can be uncomfortable; you have to hold the tank upside down and hold the valve open so air can escape through the supply tube. To eliminate the need for this procedure, many sprayers come with pressure-release valves on top of the tank. To release pressure, you pull on the valve.

Pressure-release valves often play other roles, too. Many prevent overpressurization of the tank. On most of the sprayers I examined, I couldn't see how anyone could pump enough to force the valve to blow, but a sprayer left in the sun might build up excessive pressure. Some release valves (on the Suncast GT300 and Suncast IT200, for example) also serve as gauges, allowing you to see the relative pressure in the tank (see photo on facing page).

Pressure-release valves have drawbacks. Most send chemical vapors shooting straight up in the direction of the user's face. And release valves don't clear out the hose the way inverting the tank does. As the last step in cleaning, you must be sure to drain the hose.

Satisfying your needs

Before deciding on a sprayer, assess your needs. If you don't go through more than a bottle or two of pre-mixed garden chemicals in a year, you don't need a sprayer. If you spray enough that a sprayer would sometimes come in handy, consider an inexpensive, basic model. If you spray large quantities often, then you may want a more durable model with more convenience features. Your budget may decide. Retail prices in stores vary from under $15 for the basic models to as much as $50 or more for the Cadillacs.

Whatever sprayer you choose, remember that a thorough cleaning after every use is the key to its long life. □

Chris Curless is associate editor of Fine Gardening.

Drip Tape and Microsprinklers

A simple system waters gardens of any size and shape

by Michael Maltas

When I moved to northern California in 1985, lured by an offer to create a showcase garden, I knew I'd need an irrigation system that I could adapt to ornamentals, fruits and vegetables. I eventually chose drip irrigation, which delivers water in a steady trickle, minimizing moisture fluctuations in the soil. Drip information was frustratingly scarce (and it still is), so I ended up testing almost every product on the market. I think what I learned will save you a lot of uncertainty and help you install a simple, reliable system.

My system is built around two components: drip tape and microsprinklers. Drip tape is plastic tubing with regularly spaced, built-in emitters—miniature water meters with low flow rates. Microsprinklers are spray heads 1/20 the size of ordinary sprinklers, and are sold in a variety of spray patterns. With drip tape and microsprinklers, you can water a plot of nearly any size and shape, running the tape in straight lines or slight curves and using the sprinklers to cover isolated plants. Drip tape and microsprinklers work for foundation plantings, fruit and vegetable growing, flower beds and mixed plantings, and their layout is limited only by your imagination.

Why drip?

Climate and ambition obliged me to rely on drip irrigation. My new employer, Fetzer Vineyards, wanted a garden to demonstrate the pleasures of fresh food and wine. I wanted the garden to incorporate as many fruit and vegetable varieties as possible, and that meant acreage. I also wanted it to be highly productive but easy to manage, including watering. It had to be attractive to visitors, so I planned flower beds and formal paths. The climate here, two hours north of San Francisco, is Mediterranean: wet in winter, rainless from May to September, with months of hot weather. Without irrigation, conventional gardening is impossible.

I rejected overhead watering with sprinklers, the main alternative to drip. Overhead sprinklers lose water to evapo-

Author Maltas sets out cell-pack seedlings of romaine lettuce at his demonstration garden in Hopland, California, which is irrigated largely by drip tape and microsprinklers. Here, two runs of drip tape—plastic tubing with built-in emitters at regular spacings—will wet the raised bed completely.

ration; splash dirt on plants; crust the soil surface; and wet leaves and stems, which can promote fungal diseases.

I also ruled out overhead watering in order to accommodate visitors. The site had poor drainage and heavy clay subsoil, so I planned to grow everything in raised beds, except for isolated trees, shrubs and vines. The beds would need thorough wetting every day or two during the dry months, yet the paths had to stay dry to spare people muddy feet.

Early on, I eliminated two drip systems as possibilities. Leaky hose, which is porous plastic or rubber pipe that "sweats" uniformly along its entire length, works well only when buried, and I didn't want a buried system. You have to dig trenches to install the pipe, which is a lot of work. Moreover, gophers and voles chew on buried pipe, and since you can't see it, you're bound to forget it's there and tear into it with a shovel or a weeder. Besides, buried systems are troublesome to repair, and have to be removed when you renovate beds. I also avoided the emitters that you plug into flexible plastic tubing, mainly because of labor and cost. For full wetting,

I needed emitters 8 in. apart. At that rate, the cost would be much higher than for drip tape. In addition, emitters break off easily, making maintenance a problem. I used a few emitters, mostly where I needed to curve tubing sharply or to fill in corners. The ideal garden for emitters would have comparatively widely spaced, permanent, medium-size mature plants that need more or less the same amount of water—a rose garden, for example.

Drip tape

Once I had chosen drip tape, I tested as many brands as I could ferret out. I wanted a tape that delivered water evenly, was hard to clog and easy to clean, and was relatively durable (I object to throwaway products, like drip tapes with 4-mil tubing that lasts a year at best).

Four brands stood out: Drip-In, Netafim, Chapin and T-Tape. You could use any of them with good results (see Sources, p. 42). Drip-In offers a 20-milthick wall, which makes by far the most durable drip tape available. It ought to last 15 years, with care. It can be curved fairly sharply without kinking, an advantage in some situations. I'd recommend it highly for a smaller garden, but the somewhat steep price made it impractical for me—I use thousands of feet of tape. Netafim worked well in my tests and was affordable, but it didn't have the close spacing I wanted. Both Chapin and T-Tape offered suitable spacing, good performance and reasonable price. I chose T-Tape because it was readily available on the West Coast, while Chapin, an East Coast company, had extra shipping charges. I decided on 15-mil T-Tape with emitters 8 in. apart (there are several other wall thicknesses and emitter spacings). It's designed for a water pressure of 8 psi, but I found that it held together even when I inadvertently let 50 psi go through it for a few hours. Judging by my experience so far, I think it will last three to five years.

Connectors

To assemble a drip system, you need connectors—*T*s, *L*s and splices that connect tape to tape and tape to the flexible polyethylene tubing, rigid pipe and threaded hose fittings needed to bring water to the tape. (The drawing at the bottom of p. 40 shows most of the connections you'll need.) I researched all kinds of connectors for drip tape and finally chose Loc-Eze fittings. They have a clever locking ring that works for all drip tapes and gets tighter the more you twist it. And the price is reasonable. There are other fittings that work well, too. The suppliers on p. 42 can recommend brands for most systems.

Much of my garden is laid out in 42-in.-wide raised beds, which two runs of

drip will wet fully. To supply the runs with water, and to allow me to shut off beds individually, I designed the system of connectors and ½-in. poly tubing—a manifold—shown in the photo at right. The runs are about 1 ft. apart. If a bed needs more than two runs, I just extend the manifold with more fittings.

You can readily design manifolds to suit any shape garden. The options include supplying water at one end of the manifold or in the middle; using runs of poly tubing to connect several manifolds; running tape on both sides of the manifold; and filling in corners by branching from one run to start one or more new runs. Most of the possibilities appear in the drawing on p. 41.

(Text continues on p. 42.)

Buried water pipe and a faucet allow Maltas to control his raised beds separately. Pencil rebar by the *L*s takes the strain of taut drip tape.

Drip tape adapts readily to irregularly shaped beds. Here, Maltas covers a wedge-shaped corner with *T*s and progressively shorter runs of tape. The shortest visible run is not drip tape but flexible tubing with plug-in emitters.

Basic drip-irrigation components

Component	Construction	Use	Coverage	Comments
Drip tape (Tubing with built-in emitters)	Several manufacturers and variations: emitters molded in tubing wall, piggybacked on tubing, inside tubing. Also laser-cut holes.	Above-ground straight runs or slight curves. One brand, Drip-In, tolerates tighter curves.	Available in wide range of emitter spacings and flows.	Easily installed, altered or removed.
Tubing with plug-in emitters	Many brands of plug-in emitters, including pressure-compensating and self-cleaning types.	Above-ground straight or curving runs.	Emitters available in wide range of flows. Gardener chooses spacing.	Easily altered. Adaptable to wide range of watering needs. Time-consuming and relatively expensive to insert emitters for big systems.
Porous tubing ("Leaky hose")	Spongey plastic tubing that oozes water through pores its entire length.	Must be buried in root zone for good performance. Straight or curving runs.	Spacing between runs and duration of watering control coverage.	Must be installed in separate systems for plants of differing water needs. Repair is relatively laborious.
Microsprinklers	Hard plastic inserts with precision orifices and deflectors; used atop stakes or pipe risers.	For watering isolated plants in ground or containers.	Available in spray patterns from 45° to 360° and flows from 4 gal. to 25 gal. per hour.	Fine, even spray. Deflects in wind; will not blast through foliage. Best under trees and shrubs. As plants grow, easy to replace insert with larger size.

Drip for your garden

The facing page illustrates how to lay out drip tape and microsprinklers to fit nearly any need. The large drawing shows an idealized property, with garden plots, borders, a foundation planting and small trees. Each has a drip-irrigation system composed of ½-in. polyethylene tubing to distribute water to drip tape, microsprinklers or both, which in turn supply water to the plants (see the key to identify the components). The satellite drawings show assembly options with the fittings in the drawing on this page. On rectangular plots, such as the vegetable garden, place poly tubing in the middle or at one end, and use equal-length runs of drip tape. For irregularly shaped plots, fill the corners either by branching repeatedly, as in the perennial border, or by using more than one water-supply inlet, as in the annual bed. Use microsprinklers to water isolated plants.

Start small. Pick one area, such as the foundation plantings, install a system, and learn its limits. Beyond a certain length, runs of drip tape and poly tubing lose pressure and flow. For relatively short runs, like those along the foundation, supply water at one end (as the square symbol indicates). In plots with many runs of drip tape, like the annual bed, and in plots with long drip-tape runs, like those on the right and left property lines, supply water near the middle, or split up the runs and give them separate water supplies. There are two adapters that connect drip tape to ½-in. poly tubing (see "Fittings and microsprinklers" below). The threaded adapter permits greater flow than the plug-in adapter. Use it for long and branched runs, as in drawing E on the facing page, and use the plug-in adapter for short runs, as in drawing B.

If your first system has ample capacity, you can use it to supply another system, as shown by the poly tubing linking both perennial borders. You can also splice into a system with a run of poly tubing to supply microsprinklers, as shown with the dwarf fruit trees and several accent trees. However, a long run of drip tape may lack the pressure to run microsprinklers with flows greater than 6 gal. to 10 gal. per hour. Instead of splicing into a long run, supply the microsprinklers with a separate run of poly tubing.

The drawings on the facing page are meant to show the flexibility of drip components, and are not blueprints for construction. Neither the large drawing nor the close-up views are drawn to scale.

Water supply

Drip tape and microsprinklers need clean, low-pressure water. The drawing at right shows how to assemble a water-handling system on your home's outdoor faucet. First, for convenience, attach a Y with shutoff valves. If you need automatic watering, add a battery-operated timer. Then attach a water filter of 150-mesh or finer, and a pressure regulator. (See Sources on p. 42 for the components.)

Use a garden hose or bury rigid PVC pipe to supply water to the garden. If you bury pipe, bring water to the surface with a PVC riser that ends at a hose bibb, then connect the drip-irrigation system with a hose swivel, as shown here. If you use a garden hose, connect it the same way. Compare pipe and hose before you choose. Buried pipe is harder to install, but more sightly than garden hose. If you have several drip systems, a buried pipe (and automatic timer) can serve them all, but a garden hose cannot—you'll have to move it from one system to the other.

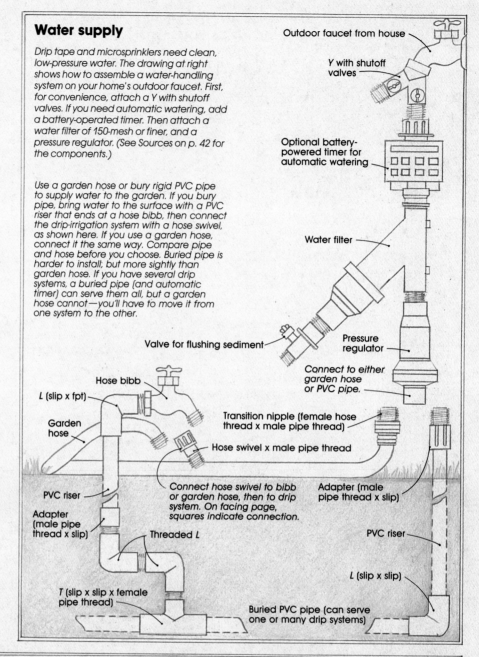

Outdoor faucet from house

Y with shutoff valves

Optional battery-powered timer for automatic watering

Water filter

Pressure regulator

Connect to either garden hose or PVC pipe.

Transition nipple (female hose thread x male pipe thread)

Hose swivel x male pipe thread

Adapter (male pipe thread x slip)

PVC riser

L (slip x slip)

Buried PVC pipe (can serve one or many drip systems)

Hose bibb

L (slip x fpt)

Garden hose

Valve for flushing sediment

PVC riser

Adapter (male pipe thread x slip)

Threaded L

T (slip x slip x female pipe thread)

Connect hose swivel to bibb or garden hose, then to drip system. On facing page, squares indicate connection.

Fittings and microsprinklers

To assemble poly tubing, drip tape and microsprinklers, you need fittings—Ts, Ls, adapters and their kin. The drip systems on the facing page go together with the fittings shown at right.

The abbreviations describe the features of each fitting. For example, "Adapter (mpt x dt)" has male pipe threads at one end and a drip-tape fastener at the other end. The abbreviation "fpt" means female iron pipe thread; "fht" means female hose thread. Compression fittings, into which you insert poly tubing, are abbreviated "c." Not shown here are barbed fittings, which you insert in poly tubing. They're interchangeable with compression fittings, but fewer kinds are available.

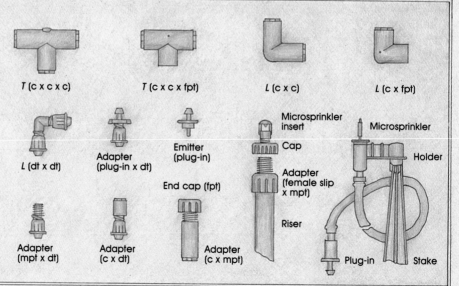

T (c x c x c)

T (c x c x fpt)

L (c x c)

L (c x fpt)

L (dt x dt)

Adapter (plug-in x dt)

Emitter (plug-in)

End cap (fpt)

Microsprinkler insert

Cap

Adapter (female slip x mpt)

Riser

Microsprinkler

Holder

Plug-in

Stake

Adapter (mpt x dt)

Adapter (c x dt)

Adapter (c x mpt)

Illustrations: Laura B. Goodwin

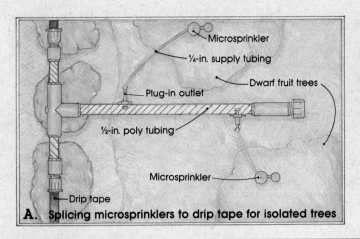

A. Splicing microsprinklers to drip tape for isolated trees

- Microsprinkler
- ¼-in. supply tubing
- Dwarf fruit trees
- Plug-in outlet
- ½-in. poly tubing
- Microsprinkler
- Drip tape

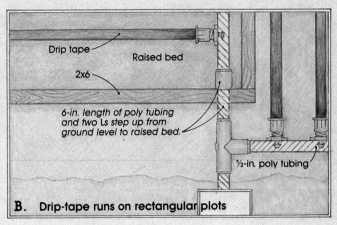

B. Drip-tape runs on rectangular plots

- Drip tape
- Raised bed
- 2x6
- 6-in. length of poly tubing and two Ls step up from ground level to raised bed.
- ½-in. poly tubing

Using drip tape and microsprinklers

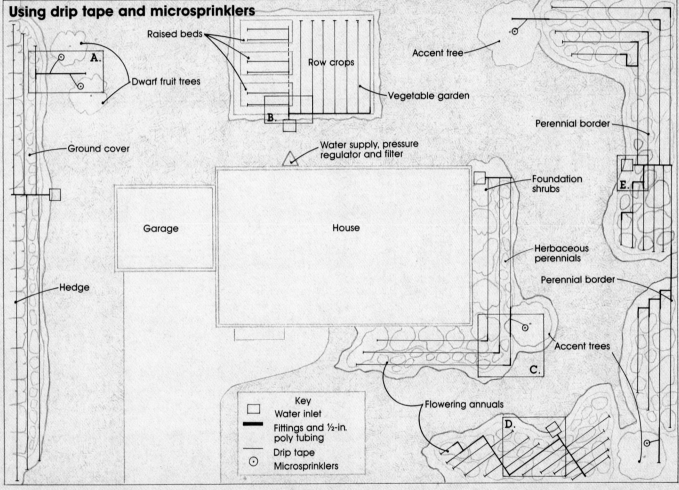

- Raised beds
- Row crops
- Accent tree
- A.
- Dwarf fruit trees
- Vegetable garden
- Perennial border
- B.
- Ground cover
- Water supply, pressure regulator and filter
- Foundation shrubs
- E.
- Garage
- House
- Herbaceous perennials
- Perennial border
- Hedge
- Accent trees
- C.
- Flowering annuals
- D.

Key
- ☐ Water inlet
- ▬ Fittings and ½-in. poly tubing
- ⊙ Drip tape
- ⊙ Microsprinklers

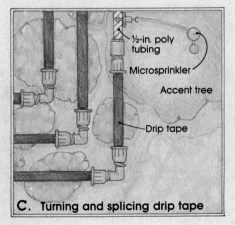

C. Turning and splicing drip tape

- ½-in. poly tubing
- Microsprinkler
- Accent tree
- Drip tape

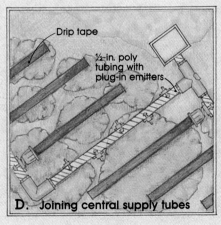

D. Joining central supply tubes

- Drip tape
- ½-in. poly tubing with plug-in emitters

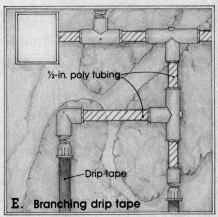

E. Branching drip tape

- ½-in. poly tubing
- Drip tape

Long runs of drip tape tend to undulate as they expand and contract with changes in temperature. To keep the tape straight, Maltas stretches it and tensions it with the crosswire and U-shaped wire anchor shown above and in the sketch.

Author's drip-tape closure

Flatten short piece of ¾-in. hose and slip over drip tape. Fold drip tape, slide hose piece over fold and insert horizontal wire. Pull drip tape taut and hold in place by driving wire hoop into soil.

¾-in. hose

12-ga. galvanized wire

Drip tape

←15-in. legs

For isolated plants, Maltas waters with microsprinklers. The white riser is a length of PVC pipe connected to a buried water line. The microsprinkler sits atop a plastic stake and sprays a 3-ft.-dia. circle.

To bring water to the garden, I buried PVC pipe with risers at each bed. I used two street Ls to connect risers to the buried pipe. The Ls are threaded, and if someone bangs a riser, they turn, preventing damage to the buried pipe. Even for a small home garden, I strongly recommend buried pipe and risers, provided your landscape is reasonably permanent. The convenience and lack of clutter are worth the work. Also, you can install a battery-powered programmable timer and automate your entire watering system. (The timers are widely available for about $50.)

You can, however, easily do without buried pipe. The simplest approach is to bring water to the drip system with a garden hose, as shown in the drawing on p. 40. You can still use a timer, but if you have more than one drip system, you'll have to move the hose.

Laying T-Tape

I chose to use the T-Tape above ground (it can also be buried), but soon discovered a problem. The longer the run, the more the T-Tape expands and contracts as it heats and cools, making it undulate like a slow-motion snake. Water goes where it doesn't belong and the tape looks messy. For short runs, under 50 ft. or so, the movement is no problem, but my runs are 100 ft. or more, so I devised a way to tension and anchor the tape. Once I have the manifold in place and the T-Tape connected to it, I head for the other end of the bed. There, I give each run of T-Tape a homemade end cap. I fold the cut end of the T-Tape and slip a short piece of tubing over the fold, forming a leak-proof closure (see the drawing above). I could buy manufactured end caps, but mine have advantages: they're easy to open (you need to flush the tape periodically to clear out sediment), they

cost almost nothing, and they're vital to my tensioning scheme. I put a 4-in. piece of 12-ga. galvanized wire in the loop of the closure, stretch the T-Tape tight, and push a U-shaped wire into the ground just in front of the straight wire. Under tension, the tape doesn't undulate. To keep the tension from bending the manifold assembly, I drive 18-in. lengths of ¼-in. pencil rebar into the ground (being sure not to hit the underground pipe) just in front of each tape connection, as shown in the top photo on p. 39.

My decision to lay T-Tape above ground makes it easy to disconnect the runs for soil work or winter storage, but it subjects the tape to deterioration from the ultraviolet component of sunlight and it makes the beds less sightly. In most beds, though, the plants are closely spaced and hide the tape much of the season. Another good camouflage

SOURCES

These mail-order suppliers carry extensive lists of drip-irrigation components, including drip tape, microsprinklers, flexible tubing, connectors, PVC pipe and fittings, water filters, pressure regulators, and automatic timers. No one supplier has all the components mentioned by the author, but all offer the range needed to assemble complete watering systems.

Harmony Farm Supply, P.O. Box 451, Graton, CA 95444. Catalog $2.00.

Plastic Plumbing Products, P.O. Box 186, Grover, MO 63040. Catalog free.

Trickle Soak Systems, 8733 Magnolia, Suite 100, Santee, CA 92071. "Homeowners' Drip Irrigation" catalog free.

The Urban Farmer Store, 2833 Vicente St., San Francisco, CA 94116. "Drip Irrigation" catalog $1.00.

would be to spread mulch once you've laid the tape.

Microsprinklers

I use microsprinklers on isolated or widely spaced trees and shrubs that I can't water economically with drip tape. One microsprinkler will water a large area, and as the plant grows I can replace the original sprinkler head with one that delivers more water. There are a few things to bear in mind about microsprinklers. They're not particularly powerful—wind can disrupt their pattern, and the fine spray will not blast through dense foliage. The patterns are always some portion of a circle, so you can't make a row of microsprinklers without dry spots and overlaps. Finally, they use more water than tape or emitters do.

Microsprinklers come in many styles, with spray patterns ranging from 45° to nearly 360°. There are two main types. One attaches to a stake, and the other plugs into an adapter that attaches to poly tubing or threaded pipe. Of the brands of microsprinklers that I tested, Ein-Tal proved best. These microsprinklers have a good self-cleaning design, and are color-coded to indicate output and diameter of spray. All Ein-Tals have 360° patterns, which limits the places they can be used. Solcoor microsprinklers also work well, and they offer spray patterns ranging from 45° to 360°. The sprinklers are quite complex, however, and the range of options is rather daunting, so my tendency is to skip to something simpler. Hardie also makes good microsprinklers, including one that splits the spray around a tree's trunk.

Microsprinklers need to be 1 ft. to 2 ft. above ground. If you use poly tubing to supply water, buy microsprinklers for stakes, and buy stakes or improvise your own. You just plug the microsprinkler's

¼-in.-dia. supply line into the supply tubing with a barbed self-sealing connector. I use plug-in microsprinklers atop ½-in.-dia. PVC risers that come up off a buried pipe. I tried several riser schemes before I got a leak-proof version. I come off the buried main with a length of PVC I.P.S. tubing, which is flexible enough to absorb a blow and to allow exact positioning of the riser. I use either of two adapters to attach microsprinklers to the risers. The Spears adapter fits onto ½-in. flexible tubing and male threaded ½-in. PVC, and has a ⅛-in.-dia. hole in the top that accepts almost all plug-in microsprinklers. The Iridelco adapter is rubberized, also fits tubing and PVC pipe, and has the advantage of adapting to a wider range of plug-in sprinklers because the hole can be enlarged.

Clean water and pressure regulation

Drip systems need clean water. At a minimum, install a good 150-mesh screen filter at the head of your system. It will trap algae and dirt and keep them from clogging emitters. I've tried several brands, and I find that filters in the $12 to $15 range do the job and repay the investment. Cheap filters (under $5) are just about worthless in my experience.

If your water source is very high in algae (a pond or a lake), I can't really recommend using it with a drip system. But if you're determined to try, use two very-fine-mesh screen filters in series and clean them daily. Regular injections of chlorine will also be needed. A siphon-suction injector will add the right amount of chlorine in 15 to 30 minutes, and chlorine volatilizes so quickly that it doesn't hurt the plants at all.

Drip components are designed for low water pressure. They will malfunction and break with normal household pressure, which is 40 psi to 60 psi. You must step it down to 8 psi to 15 psi with a pressure regulator. Buy a good one. The cheap brands break regularly.

Experiments ahead

My experience with drip tape and microsprinklers has been so positive that I'm using them for almost every plant in the garden, from dwarf fruit trees on down. I'm still enlarging the garden and experimenting with the drip system, so my opinions change about what works best. But the great advantage to the system I've cobbled up is that almost all the above-ground parts are interchangeable, so the design is flexible enough to change with me. ☐

Michael Maltas's demonstration garden is at the Valley Oaks Food and Wine Center of Fetzer Vineyards in Hopland, California.

Michael Maltas stands at one corner of his remarkable demonstration garden.

Perfectionist by Jill Hannum

Michael Maltas has made a garden that leaves first-time visitors groping for adjectives. I don't think there's anything like it anywhere else in the United States: 4½ acres of seemingly flawless horticulture laid out in raised beds between fastidiously groomed paths; wide English-type perennial borders and small flower plots interspersed with rows and rows of produce in long beds tailored for maximum production; and everything planted more densely than I've ever seen before. Lush and productive, the garden belies the seasonal heat and drought of northern California, where no rain falls six months of the year.

Maltas calls the garden a compromise between a big production field and an English country garden. It does somehow look both efficient and welcoming, though the welcome is very formal. This is your wealthy aunt's gracious home where you're free to wander around and look to your heart's content as long as you don't get too laid back about it. Maltas is a stickler for precision and detail. Ask him about varieties, performance, pruning, rootstock, anything at all, and he pulls out a thick file detailing his experiments and trials. He studied at Emerson College in England, where the focus is on the teachings of Rudolf Steiner, founder of biodynamics, a horticultural system baffling to outsiders, especially the herbal extracts that purportedly speed composting and suppress plant diseases. I suspect, though, that Maltas succeeds more on temperament—his drive for perfection—than on training.

The garden awes and unsettles me. It's a commercial enterprise, initiated by Fetzer Vineyards as a showpiece and source of first-rate produce for their Valley Oaks Food and Wine Center, restaurant, and small grocery store. It's also meant to attract publicity, and it does. On the other hand,

the garden is the antithesis of commercial agriculture—especially California agriculture—which produces cosmetically perfect produce with an arsenal of pesticides. Maltas uses no synthetic pesticides or fertilizers, yet the garden is jammed with healthy plants. There are no weeds, the paths are raked clean, even the blue jays seem to respect the fruit. I boggle at his success, but he takes it for granted. When we discussed the virtues of his produce, he stressed flavor and variety. When I said, yes, but it's also unpoisoned and more nutritious, he looked briefly befuddled, as if my point were too obvious to mention. If I had my way, there'd be a banner at the entrance that said "Organic!"

Maltas is a self-described "varieties fanatic." He says that a visitor who sees and tastes 20 kinds of lettuce will learn that there's more to life than iceberg. There are over 1,000 varieties grown at Valley Oaks each year, many for the first and last time. If something doesn't thrive or proves vulnerable to pests, it comes out, even if "it" is a whole row of four-year-old trees whose rootstock suckers too much. Maltas says that the garden will be easier to run when he no longer plants, labels and evaluates 54 kinds of tomatoes and 46 of melons, but he still plans to grow hundreds of the best varieties.

Someday I'll ask him what kind of garden he'd create if he had no one to please but himself. I need a little randomness (maybe sloppiness is the word) to feel comfortable, but I don't think Maltas is comfortable until all the slop is eliminated. His ideal garden might be very different from Valley Oaks, but it would be done absolutely right. ☐

Jill Hannum gardens in the hills near Yorkville, California, a short hop and long drive from Michael Maltas's garden in Hopland.

Drip-Irrigation Basics
A homemade system for a small orchard

Layout of Kourik's system

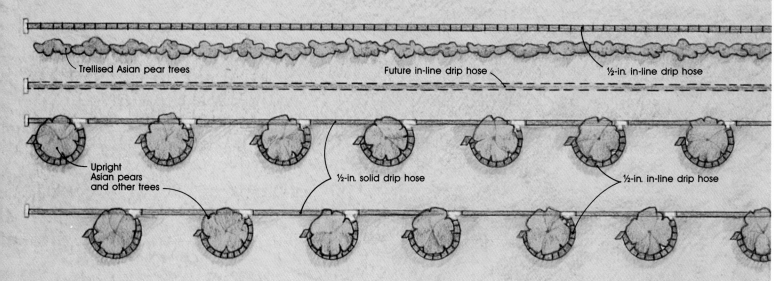

Trellised Asian pear trees

Future in-line drip hose

½-in. in-line drip hose

Upright Asian pears and other trees

½-in. solid drip hose

½-in. in-line drip hose

by Robert Kourik

Recent droughts and water shortages have focused attention on water-saving gardening practices and irrigation systems. I think that drip irrigation, a low-volume, low-pressure system that delivers water directly to plant roots instead of losing it to the air, is often your best bet. When used regularly, it minimizes water stress in plants and almost always increases yields. I've found that it's ideal for fruit trees and ornamental plantings of trees and shrubs. I can best explain the basics by telling you about a drip-irrigation system I installed in a small plot of Asian pear trees I planted about five years ago.

The orchard is on my friend Chester Aaron's property in Occidental, California, about four miles from my home. I'd grown Asian pears before, having developed a craving for their potent, complex flavor and perfume, and I knew that they thrive when watered during the California dry season, from about May through September. Like most fruit trees, Asian pears can survive without summer irrigation once they're established, but fruit yields and quality decrease. I'd have to water my trees from Chester's well, which might recharge slowly and run dry during droughts. I promised Chester that the drip system I planned would never threaten his water supply.

In a drip system, water flows through flexible plastic tubing and dribbles out small emitters on or just beneath the soil surface. The trunks and canopies of my trees stay dry, creating an inhospitable environment for fungal diseases and fire blight, which, for pear trees in particular, is a potentially lethal bacterial disease. By using emitters that release as little as ½ gal. of water per hour, my entire system uses less water in a day than a sprinkler uses in an hour. I laid out the drip hose in two patterns, both suitable for watering fruit trees in the sandy loam of this region: straight lines next to closely spaced, trellised trees, and circles around more widely spaced, freestanding, upright trees.

Several companies sell complete drip kits, but I prefer to put my own system together. This approach allows me to design the most efficient and suitable system for my site. Various drip-irrigation parts are made by different manufacturers, but I was able to purchase everything I needed from Harmony Farm Supply (see Sources, p. 49). The basic component of my drip system is flexible, ½-in. polyethylene in-line drip hose with tortuous-path emitters that are pre-installed in the hose by the manufacturer. (When I built my system, hose was available only in 1,000-ft. rolls; today you can get it in 100-ft. rolls.) Water under low pressure moves through the labyrinth-like passages in each emitter and trickles out a tiny opening in the hose wall, as shown in the drawing on the facing page. The turns inside the emitter create turbulence so that any dirt in the water won't settle out and clog the emitter. I prefer in-line drip hose to drip tape (thin tubing with numerous pinholes along its length), which easily clogs, kinks and breaks,

Illustrations, except where noted: Laura B. Goodwin

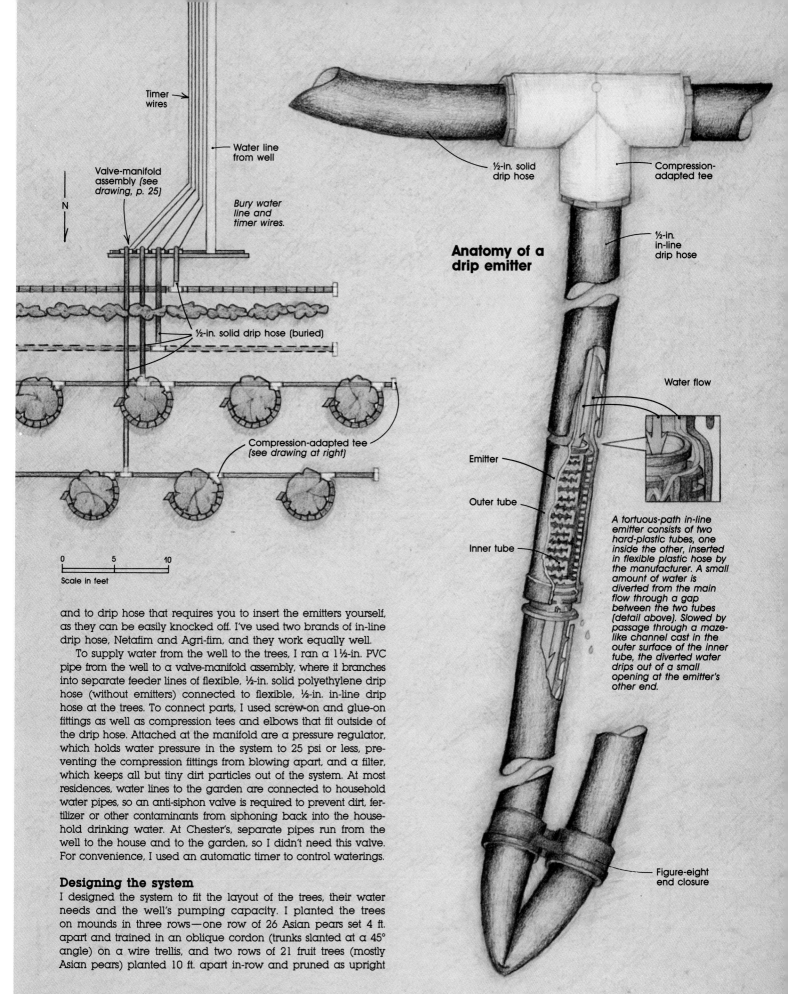

Timer wires

Water line from well

Valve-manifold assembly *(see drawing, p. 25)*

N

Bury water line and timer wires.

½-in. solid drip hose (buried)

Compression-adapted tee *(see drawing at right)*

0   5   10
Scale in feet

Anatomy of a drip emitter

½-in. solid drip hose

Compression-adapted tee

½-in. in-line drip hose

Water flow

Emitter

Outer tube

Inner tube

A tortuous-path in-line emitter consists of two hard-plastic tubes, one inside the other, inserted in flexible plastic hose by the manufacturer. A small amount of water is diverted from the main flow through a gap between the two tubes (detail above). Slowed by passage through a maze-like channel cast in the outer surface of the inner tube, the diverted water drips out of a small opening at the emitter's other end.

Figure-eight end closure

and to drip hose that requires you to insert the emitters yourself, as they can be easily knocked off. I've used two brands of in-line drip hose, Netafim and Agri-fim, and they work equally well.

To supply water from the well to the trees, I ran a 1½-in. PVC pipe from the well to a valve-manifold assembly, where it branches into separate feeder lines of flexible, ½-in. solid polyethylene drip hose (without emitters) connected to flexible, ½-in. in-line drip hose at the trees. To connect parts, I used screw-on and glue-on fittings as well as compression tees and elbows that fit outside of the drip hose. Attached at the manifold are a pressure regulator, which holds water pressure in the system to 25 psi or less, preventing the compression fittings from blowing apart, and a filter, which keeps all but tiny dirt particles out of the system. At most residences, water lines to the garden are connected to household water pipes, so an anti-siphon valve is required to prevent dirt, fertilizer or other contaminants from siphoning back into the household drinking water. At Chester's, separate pipes run from the well to the house and to the garden, so I didn't need this valve. For convenience, I used an automatic timer to control waterings.

Designing the system

I designed the system to fit the layout of the trees, their water needs and the well's pumping capacity. I planted the trees on mounds in three rows—one row of 26 Asian pears set 4 ft. apart and trained in an oblique cordon (trunks slanted at a 45° angle) on a wire trellis, and two rows of 21 fruit trees (mostly Asian pears) planted 10 ft. apart in-row and pruned as upright

Kourik installed a drip-irrigation system to water his plot of Asian pear trees in northern California. The system conserved water, placed a modest demand on his well, avoided water-borne diseases and produced a bumper crop of fruit. The unobtrusive system would be ideal for ornamental plantings, too.

trees. Ideally, I think it's best to irrigate a doughnut-shaped ring of soil on the soil surface at or just beyond the dripline of each tree. In sandy loam, each emitter wets a carrot-shaped volume of soil beneath the surface (see drawing, p. 48), and together the emitters keep the upper 2 ft. to 3 ft. of soil moist. The dripline is directly beneath the outer edge of a tree's canopy, an area where many root hairs and feeder roots grow. Watering there encourages roots to grow outward, anchoring the tree.

I decided to lay a line of solid drip hose alongside each row of upright trees and connect it to a loop of in-line drip hose encircling each tree. Looping 12 ft. of hose would be enough for small trees, and as the trees grew I could enlarge the loops. I assumed that the trellised trees would do fine with just one in-line drip hose along the side of the row. Their growth would be restricted by the close planting, and I thought the carrot-shaped wetting pattern would reach enough of their root system. Later on, I'd add a line on the other side of the trellis.

Water needs—To find out how much water my trees would need, I first called the local Cooperative Extension office to get the evapo-transpiration (ET) rate for trees grown in my climate. The ET rate is the amount of water, usually calculated in inches per day, that evaporates from a specified area of soil surface and transpires from plants growing there. This rate is then translated into the minimum amount of water required just to keep up with water losses. (Although different plants have different ET values, one rate is usually given for all plants in an area.)

For my area, the average ET rate during a typical summer is 0.10 in. per day or 3 in. per month. Using a chart supplied by the Extension Service (shown on the facing page), I calculated the daily water use for mature trees so that the system wouldn't fall short as the trees grew. Rounding the figure for an acre of solid plant cover to 3,000 gal. per day, I determined that my 1/10 acre of closely spaced trees would need 300 gal. per day when mature; that's about 6½ gal. per day for each of the 47 trees.

Next I calculated the number of emitters I'd need. In-line drip hose can be purchased with emitters of different flow capacities and with various intervals between the emitters. The total capacity of emitters that are run at the same time can't exceed the capacity of the hose—at 25 psi, this is 235 gal. per hour. To minimize the amount of water I'd pump at one time, I decided to use the smallest-capacity emitters, which release ½ gal. of water per hour. At this rate, theoretically I could run up to 470 emitters at one time.

I chose drip hose with emitters spaced 12 in. apart. (Emitters in a clay soil can be farther apart.) At this spacing, I could run a line 470 ft. long, much longer than my layout required. I'd initially need in-line hose with 352 emitters for the entire planting— 12 emitters in the loop of hose around each upright tree and about 100 in the 100-ft. hose alongside the trellised trees. If I wanted to irrigate through all the lines at the same time, I'd need a water supply of 176 gal. per hour.

Chester's records showed the well's flow rate (that is, the maximum amount of water that the well could continuously deliver without running dry) to be 4 gal. per minute or 240 gal. per hour. If I irrigated round the clock at that rate, theoretically I could supply 5,760 gal. per day, much more than was needed to compensate for the ET loss of 300 gal. per day. (Flow rates for wells should be available from the drilling company. I never check city water supplies—they're almost always ample. If you're curious about how much water your municipal system can deliver, clock how long it takes to fill a 5-gal. bucket from a hose bibb, making sure that no other faucets are open at the time. For example, 10 minutes to fill the bucket equals a flow rate of 30 gal. per hour.)

Filter and valves—Even though in-line hose is designed to prevent dirty water from clogging the emitters, I always install a filter, even with city water. I prefer Y-type filters over the less expensive, in-line hose filters. The Y-filters have a greater water-flow capacity and are much easier to clean. Water comes into the filter, spins around in a cylinder, and passes through a metal mesh screen and then through the valve assembly into the drip hose.

I chose a Y-filter with a flow capacity of 660 gal. per hour and a 200-mesh metal screen. A large filter doesn't need cleaning as often; a 200-mesh screen is the smallest available. Well water or dirty water requires 150- to 200-mesh, while clean city water requires 80- to 120-mesh. Metal screens are much sturdier and easier to clean than nylon ones are.

For the first few years, I'd be able to run the entire system all at once, but eventually the water needs of the trees would exceed the flow rate of the well as well as the capacity of the hose. So I decided to divide the system into four lines, each controlled by a separate valve. I'd use two initially, then use the other two as the trees grew and water needs increased.

Irrigation schedule—Finally, I worked out a tentative irrigation schedule for the first year based on the water requirements of a one-year-old fruit tree. I could maximize growth during the trees'

DAILY WATER NEEDS OF PLANTS

Sq. ft. of plant cover	ET (Evapo-transpiration rate in in./day)*			
	0.10	0.20	0.25	0.30
	DAILY WATER USE (gal./day)			
4 sq. ft. (1-yr.-old fruit tree)	0.25	0.50	0.62	0.75
10 sq. ft. (2-yr.-old fruit tree)	0.62	1.25	1.56	1.87
100 sq. ft. (4-yr.-old fruit tree)	6.2	12.5	15.6	18.7
1 acre solid cover	2,715	5,431	6,788	8,146

The ET rate in a given climate takes into account factors such as temperature, precipitation, wind conditions and season. Consult your local Cooperative Extension Service for the ET rate in your area.

Valve-manifold assembly

The valve manifold directs water from the main supply (at far right in the drawing) through a filter to four irrigation lines in Kourik's orchard. Each irrigation line is served by a valve assembly—valve, pressure regulator, hose swivel and connecting parts, as shown at left below. An electronic timer opens and closes the valves according to a programmed schedule. The photo at right shows Kourik's setup, the four valve assemblies connected by short nipple sections.

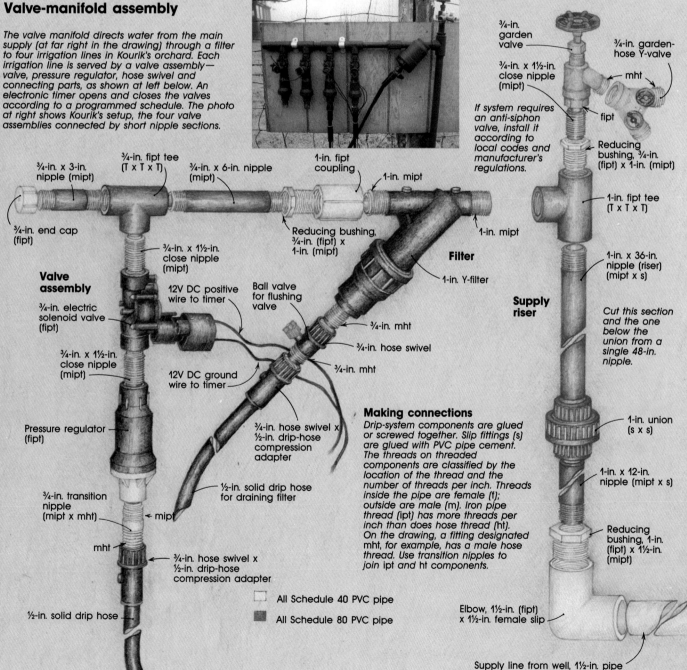

If system requires an anti-siphon valve, install it according to local codes and manufacturer's regulations.

¾-in. garden valve

¾-in. garden-hose Y-valve

¾-in. x 1½-in. close nipple (mipt)

mht

fipt

Reducing bushing, ¾-in. (fipt) x 1-in. (mipt)

1-in. fipt tee (T x T x T)

1-in. x 36-in. nipple (riser) (mipt x s)

Supply riser

Cut this section and the one below the union from a single 48-in. nipple.

1-in. union (s x s)

1-in. x 12-in. nipple (mipt x s)

Reducing bushing, 1-in. (fipt) x 1½-in. (mipt)

Elbow, 1½-in. (fipt) x 1½-in. female slip

Supply line from well, 1½-in. pipe

¾-in. x 3-in. nipple (mipt)

¾-in. fipt tee (T x T x T)

¾-in. x 6-in. nipple (mipt)

1-in. fipt coupling

1-in. mipt

¾-in. end cap (fipt)

¾-in. x 1½-in. close nipple (mipt)

Reducing bushing, ¾-in. (fipt) x 1-in. (mipt)

1-in. mipt

Filter

1-in. Y-filter

Valve assembly

¾-in. electric solenoid valve (fipt)

12V DC positive wire to timer

Ball valve for flushing valve

¾-in. mht

¾-in. hose swivel

¾-in. x 1½-in. close nipple (mipt)

12V DC ground wire to timer

¾-in. mht

Pressure regulator (fipt)

¾-in. hose swivel x ½-in. drip-hose compression adapter

½-in. solid drip hose for draining filter

¾-in. transition nipple (mipt x mht)

mipt

mht

¾-in. hose swivel x ½-in. drip-hose compression adapter

½-in. solid drip hose

Making connections

Drip-system components are glued or screwed together. Slip fittings (s) are glued with PVC pipe cement. The threads on threaded components are classified by the location of the thread and the number of threads per inch. Threads inside the pipe are female (f); outside are male (m). Iron pipe thread (ipt) has more threads per inch than does hose thread (ht). On the drawing, a fitting designated mht, for example, has a male hose thread. Use transition nipples to join ipt and ht components.

☐ All Schedule 40 PVC pipe

■ All Schedule 80 PVC pipe

To water the upright trees (photo at left), Kourik connected a solid drip hose from the valve manifold to another line of solid drip hose, strung from tree to tree. A loop of in-line drip hose (attached with the white tee on the left in the photo) irrigates each tree around the dripline through tiny emitter openings in the hose wall. Hanging the solid hose in the trees and temporarily lifting the loops makes mowing weeds easy. In-line drip hose alongside the row of closely spaced trellised trees (above) provides water about 18 in. from their trunks. As the trees grow, Kourik will add another line of in-line drip hose on the opposite side of the trellised trees and increase the length of the loops around the upright trees.

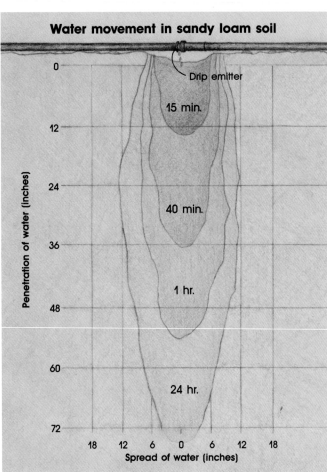

Water movement in sandy loam soil

Drip emitter

15 min.

40 min.

1 hr.

24 hr.

Penetration of water (inches)

Spread of water (inches)

formative years by applying more water than required to re-place ET losses, so I greatly increased the water-use recommen-dation of ¾ gal. per day for newly planted trees growing in stressful conditions (ET rate of 0.30 in./day) to a little more than 2 gal. per day per tree, or 15 gal. per week. I wasn't worried about waterlogging the soil because the sandy-loam mounds drained well and I would check the trees for signs of excess wa-ter. Irrigating each tree with 5 gal. three times per week would maintain even moisture, stress the trees less and place less de-mand on the well. Fifty minutes on each loop and 1¼ hours for the trellis line would do the job. A timer would allow me to irri-gate between 2:00 a.m. and 3:30 a.m., allowing the well to re-charge before Chester's morning shower.

Installation

Chester and I dug a 12-in.-deep trench from the well to the manifold location for the PVC water supply pipe and timer wires, then joined lengths of this rigid pipe and fittings with Weld-on PVC pipe cement. A large-diameter pipe delivers lots of water with minimal loss of pressure over long distances. Irrigation suppli-ers have charts for figuring correct pipe size—see "Waterworks" on pp. 50-55, for more on pipe sizing.

I bought a microchip-controlled, programmable electronic tim-er with four separate control circuits that could be switched on and off several times a week, and installed it on Chester's house. The timer cost $60, but it's worth it—cheaper ones can't be pro-grammed for as many waterings per week. I enclosed mine in a metal outdoor electrical box, rather than paying even more for

Illustration: Adapted from Buckman and Brady, *Nature and Properties of Soils*, p. 185

a waterproof device. After I ran wires from the timer to the valve manifold, I covered them and the water pipe with scrap wood and backfilled with soil. The scrap wood will alert anyone digging in the landscape to proceed with caution.

Manifold assembly—Next I assembled the valve manifold in my shop, as shown in the drawing on p. 47. I prefer the convenience of working inside, although sometimes I plumb everything on site. My tools were simple: two pipe wrenches and a workbench. Before connecting the threaded fittings, I wrapped them with Teflon tape to make a watertight seal. A thin coating of Teflon pipe dope will work, too. Just make sure it's Teflon pipe dope; other kinds will slowly eat away the plastic.

I worked up from the supply riser and firmly wrench-tightened each joint except those connecting the filter and pressure regulator. Unlike PVC fittings, which tolerate a fair amount of torque, some brands of these connections have thin-walled threads and must only be hand-tightened.

Filters with metal screens work best with full water pressure, usually 40 psi to 60 psi, so I put mine before the pressure regulator. (In-line hose filters require reduced pressure and should be attached after the pressure regulator.) If a tee that led to a valve didn't point straight down, I tightened it rather than backing it off, which would have created a leaky seal. If you need an anti-siphon valve, attach it at least 6 in. higher than the highest elevated emitter in the entire system.

Laying the drip lines—Moving to the site, I propped up the manifold near the trees and attached the riser to the water supply pipe. Screwing the assembled manifold onto the supply line would have been impossible, so I connected it with a union. A collar on the union tightens down on the riser as the collar is turned. Then I mounted the manifold on a plywood board with galvanized U-brackets. Once everything was in place, I attached a solid drip hose to the filter to pipe away water when I cleaned it.

After wiring the timer to the valves, I programmed it to turn on each line in sequence and ran it through a quick cycle to make sure everything was connected properly. Then I recorded the timer's station numbers and their corresponding drip lines.

Finally, I was ready to hook up the feeder lines and in-line drip hoses. I cut them with pruning shears. If I'm cutting hose in the hot sun, I cut it about 1½ ft. longer per 100 ft. of hose than I need, to allow for shrinkage when the temperature drops. I attached a feeder line of solid drip hose to each pressure-regulator fitting, running the hose in a trench to a point near each row of trees, then I buried all but the ends. I didn't bury the lines from there on because dirt can get stuck in the in-line hose openings and gophers will chew holes through polyethylene hose. (During the rest of the installation, each time I added more hose I manually turned on the water for five minutes to flush out the new section.)

Connecting the solid drip feeder lines to the in-line drip hoses was a little tricky. Because different manufacturers make them, solid drip hose is slightly larger in diameter than in-line hose, so compression adapters are required to fit them together.

At each upright tree, I inserted the solid drip hose into a compression-adapted tee and attached a loop of in-line drip hose, placing the loop around the tree's dripline. Once all the loops were installed, I closed off the open ends of the loops with figure-eight closures, with the water running to flush the system. (I started at the lowest point of the system—where the flow will be the greatest—and worked uphill from there.) To attach a closure, I slid one of its loops over the hose to about 18 in. from the hose end. Then I bent the hose back about 6 in. from the end to crimp it shut, and slid the closure toward the bend, hooking the open end of the hose through the other loop. Finally, I ran water through the entire system to check for leaks and clogged emitters.

Maintenance

Without proper maintenance, drip irrigation is worthless. In-line emitters don't clog easily, but I still inspect the entire system regularly. Before I turn on the timer in the spring, I look for lines that have been broken or damaged by freezing, gophers or heavy feet. I also take the filter apart, scrub the screen, and soak it in a solution of 10% chlorine bleach and water. Then I flush it out, along with the lines. During the growing season, I flush out the filter every week or two, merely turning the handle of a small built-in valve to do so. I periodically dig around the trees to make sure the soil is moist but not sopping wet—a handful of soil should crumble easily when tapped with the back of a trowel. I probably spend less than ten hours each year on maintenance.

Drip hose will supposedly last for ten years when exposed to the sun. I paint all exposed PVC plastic parts with exterior latex paint to protect them from getting brittle from sunlight exposure. Drip hose can be left outdoors year round, even in cold climates—water in the lines will dribble out of the emitters, and the hose is flexible enough to expand even if water freezes in it. To be safe, you could drain the lines before the onset of cold weather.

During the first summer, I soon was fed up with moving the hose and loops each time I mowed the weeds beneath the upright trees, so I hung the solid hose in the branches and lifted the loops when I mowed. Once the hose was elevated, the loops no longer reached around the entire dripline, but they still wet enough soil.

I was glad that I had put in extra valves. When I tried to run the whole system at once, water pressure dropped wherever the hose didn't lie straight and flat—at the tees, the loops and especially toward the uphill end of the plot. To remedy this, I used the valves to stagger the watering and I watered for less time. In-line emitters specifically designed to compensate for pressure loss probably would have solved the problem, but they weren't available at that time.

I'm very pleased with my drip system. All the trees grew about 3 ft. to 5 ft. the first year, more than I expected, and they've continued to grow vigorously and fruit prolifically, even when I had to reduce the frequency of watering during last summer's drought. I'm sure sprinkler-irrigated trees would have been leggy and harder to care for, and unirrigated trees would have yielded half as much fruit.

The hardware for my system cost $600 in 1984: $60 for the timer, $22 for wire, $150 for the valve assembly, $26 for 300 ft. of solid drip hose, $275 for 1,000 ft. of in-line drip hose, $32 for compression-adapted tees and $35 for miscellaneous fittings. Despite the initial cost and work to set it up, the system has more than repaid me. I don't spend the summer moving sprinklers and I don't worry about my water supply running out. Instead, I just relax under my trees, munching Asian pears and thinking about the gourmet restaurants that are begging to pay top dollar for all the fruit Chester and I can grow. □

Robert Kourik is a landscape designer in Occidental, California. He's currently working on a book about drip irrigation.

SOURCES

Harmony Farm Supply,
P.O. Box 451, Graton, CA 95444.
707-823-9125. Catalog $2.00.

Plastic Plumbing Products, Inc.,
17005 Manchester Rd.,
P.O. Box 186, Grover, MO 63040.
314-458-2226. Catalog $1.00.

Raindrip, Inc., P.O. Box 2173,
Chatsworth, CA 91313.
800-222-3747. Catalog free.

The Urban Farmer Store,
2833 Vicente St., San Francisco,
CA 94116. 415-661-2204.
Catalog $1.00.

The following manufacturers of in-line emitter hose sell wholesale only and can supply your local plumbing or hardware store:

Agri-fim Irrigation Products, Inc.,
1279 West Moraga Ave., Fresno,
CA 93711. 219-431-2003. Call for referral to local dealer.

Netafim Irrigation, Inc.,
104 South Central Ave.,
Valley Stream, NY 11580.
516-561-6650.

Waterworks

Installing an irrigation system
so it grows with the garden

by Dave Rodgers

When we purchased our new home four years ago, I launched a gardening program with the intent of turning a half acre of neglected, overgrown land in the hills of Oakland, California, into my private vision of horticulture splendor. Today, I'm a long way from where I was, though not yet where I want to be. I have solved one basic problem, however—that of providing water.

In Oakland, rain is essentially nonexistent from mid-May until mid-November. As I reclaimed more and more of the land, I was soon spending more than half of my gardening time watering, and even then some of my favorite things began to die. It was obvious that I needed a watering system. I'd long been planning one, but I was still experimenting with the garden layout, and the sprinkler-system plans kept changing as fast as the landscape did. In addition, our water is expensive, so I wanted to make sure I put it where it would count. Though I hesitated to commit myself to what seemed the permanence and inflexibility of an underground system, things were getting desperate, so I finally decided to see what I could do.

I had always planned to do the work myself, and it now occurred to me that not only would this save money, but it would allow me to design and install the system a little at a time, providing the flexibility I needed. I could set up the major elements to handle what I anticipated would be the long-term needs of the yard and garden. Then, using temporary setups in each area, I could test to determine specific needs before installing permanent fixtures. As the garden changed and expanded, so could my watering system. The system that has evolved is shown in the drawing on p. 54. Underground plastic pipe brings city water from the street to three valve manifolds in the yard and garden. Additional underground pipe or above-ground hoses run from the manifolds to sprinkler heads or hose bibs (outdoor faucets) that water the garden. A computerized timer oversees the operation. So far, the system has cost me about $600.

When I started, I collected all the free brochures I could get from the manufacturers of sprinkler-system components, and I suggest you do the same. (If you want to burrow deeply into the subject, you might look at James A. Watkins' *Turf Irrigation Manual*, $28.95 from Telsco Industries, P.O. Box 18205, Dallas, TX 75218.) But, while the brochures offer good basic design information, almost all of them present an oversimplified picture of what it takes to put together even a moderate system. The following outlines what I've learned putting my system together.

Planning

For me, planning was the hard part, requiring 90% of the effort (but also providing 50% of the gratification). I first had to decide what kind of delivery system I wanted: conventional overhead watering, or the newer technology of drip irrigation. Drip systems run at much lower pressure and flow than a system of overhead sprinklers, and they can therefore use a less expensive, easier-to-lay flexible plastic pipe. But I was unsure of a drip system's reliability and unsatisfied that it would provide adequate coverage for other than spot watering. I decided to install overhead watering, with impulse sprinklers, which deliver a rotating jet of water, and spray heads, which don't rotate and cover less area. By adding pressure reducers and filters later on, I could integrate drip into the system. (Most municipalities have codes governing the installation of sprinkler systems. Early on, you should check the codes with the appropriate local agency.)

Next I had to choose whether to operate the system manually or to install automatic timers. As my first priority was to free myself from watering chores, my first purchase was the fanciest computerized timer I could find (see sidebar at right). For smaller yards, the added expense and effort of automating might not make sense. You can always automate later, too, by running control wires to the valves and replacing the manual valve stems with automatic ones. (You might anticipate future automation by laying the control wires when you lay the pipe.)

Selecting pipe was straightforward. Plastic pipe, galvanized-steel pipe and copper tube all have a place in most systems, but most of the pipe you'll need will be buried underground and that can be plastic. (See the sidebar on p. 52 for more on choosing and assembling pipe.) Inexpensive and easy to work with, plastic pipe also lends itself to reconfiguration if you make mistakes or change plans. I began using plastic above and below ground, but later switched to galvanized steel and copper for the third valve manifold—metal pipe will not deteriorate in the sun or crack when tripped over in the dark.

To be effective, an irrigation system must deliver water to the sprinklers at an adequate flow and pressure. Thus you need to minimize losses of pressure (called pressure drops) in the system, which reduce the available flow to the sprinkler heads. Pipe size, valve size and flow rate

Timers

Automatic timers are either mechanical or electronic. Mechanical ones are less expensive ($30 to $45), but are severely limited in flexibility of programming. Electronic timers cost a little more ($45 to $75), but their extra features are well worth it. Either type usually can control four or six zones. If you need more zones, you can add more timers.

I bought the most flexible timer I could find, a Lawn Genie model R416LCD, which cost $56 at a discount hardware store. It is a six-zone controller, each zone consisting of one valve or two valves (two valves in one zone receive the same signal). The system allows zones to be operated on different days, selected either by days of the week (for example, every Monday, Wednesday and Saturday) or in increments of days (every day, every two days, etc.). Each zone can be programmed to water for from one minute to 13 hours in one-minute increments. (Many timers are limited to much shorter watering periods.) The system can be programmed for up to four starting times a day, but these times can't be varied by zone. When two or more zones are programmed for the same day, they run in sequence from the beginning of each start time in order of zone number.

Here's an example for two zones. Zone one is set for Monday and Wednesday, and a watering period of ten minutes. Zone two runs Tuesday and Wednesday, and its period is 40 minutes. The system's starting times are programmed at noon, 6:00 p.m. and midnight. On Monday, only zone one operates, watering for ten minutes at each starting time. On Tuesday, zone two delivers 40 minutes of water at noon, six and midnight. On Wednesday, both zones operate. At noon, zone one runs for ten minutes and shuts down, then zone two comes on for 40 minutes. Likewise at six and midnight. You can't make zone one (or any zone) water for ten minutes at noon, 15 minutes at six and 20 minutes at midnight. Likewise, on Wednesday, both zones must water at each of the programmed starting times; you can't make zone two skip the 6:00 p.m. session, for example.

You can operate the system manually, too, and interrupt the programming with a "pause" button for short periods or a "rain" button for indefinite periods. The timer's included transformer plugs directly into a 110-volt outlet, and a 9-volt battery protects the programming if power is interrupted. If your water comes from a well or a tank, an optional feature can start a pump relay anytime a valve is opened.

For easy access, I installed the timer in the stairwell leading to the basement, then ran a seven-conductor control cable (six control lines and one ground line) from the timer to a terminal strip easily reached from outside so I wouldn't have to snake wire for each valve through the house to the timer. I ran twisted-pair bell wire directly from the terminal strip to each valve near the house. To service existing and future remote valves, I ran two 7-conductor control cables from the terminal strip along the main pipeline as I laid it in the trench, attaching the cables to the pipe with nylon cable ties at 3-ft. intervals. The two-wire connections (live and ground) to each valve are made with twist-on wire nuts, filled with silicone sealant for weatherproofing. —D.R.

Impulse sprinklers attached by garden hose to an underground main line give Dave Rodgers' system flexibility (facing page).

Rodgers' hand-dug main-line trenches snake through terrace walls.

Backflow prevention

The most common municipal-code requirement for irrigation systems is for backflow prevention, to keep water in the sprinkler lines from being sucked back into the public water system. In Oakland, there are two ways to satisfy this code. In the first, if a backflow preventer is installed more than 6 in. higher than all of the line it services, it can be a simple, vacuum anti-siphon type. These are built into most plastic valves; I used them for my first two manifolds. Plastic anti-siphon valves are inexpensive; metal ones cost about three times as much. (My Lawn Genie valves cost $16 apiece at a discount hardware store. If you can't find a local supplier, call Lawn Genie at 1-800-742-4335.) Each anti-siphon valve must meet the height stipulation and each installation involves an awkward 180° loop of pipe. I've had trouble with the height requirement, so I've decided to switch to the other method allowed by code and isolate the entire system with a single, large anti-siphon device on the main service line, placed high enough to clear the entire system. This way, for the rest of the system I can use non-anti-siphon valves, which are simpler and easier to install. (I bought Champion brass valves. For a local supplier, call Constance Condon at 1-800-332-4267.) If you can't install a backflow preventer higher than all the serviced line, you'll need a much more expensive RPVB (reduced pressure vacuum breaker) device. A 1-in. RPVB can cost more than $200, but can isolate an entire system from any level.   —D.R.

Pipe

Plastic pipe is inexpensive, it doesn't rust or rot, and its polished interior surface offers the least resistance to water flow of any piping material. Two kinds are used for irrigation: polyvinyl chloride (PVC) and polyethylene (PE). PE must be assembled with fittings, not solvent, and it has much lower pressure ratings than PVC, so it can't be used for pressurized main-line runs.

Tough and durable, PVC pipe has been used successfully in irrigation systems since the 1940s. It will deteriorate when exposed over long periods to sunlight. Oakland requires all exposed plastic pipe to be wrapped with 4-mil opaque plastic tape to protect it. (Plastic valves don't need wrapping.) I buy Schedule 40 PVC pipe, which is standard for home installations, at a discount hardware store. (The Schedule number indicates pipe-wall thickness.) A 20-ft. length of 1¼-in. pipe costs me about $4; most fittings are $.60 to $1.25 each.

PVC pipe can be cut with a variety of tools: wheeled pipe cutters, hacksaws, and special-purpose, ratcheted, knife-blade pipe cutters. For me, an $8 ratcheted pipe cutter was the best for pipe ¾ in. and under, not consistently effective for 1-in. pipe (short pieces tended to break), and of no use at all for the 1¼-in. pipe, which I cut with a hacksaw.

Most plastic-pipe connections can be made with slip fittings and solvent cement (available with the pipe). Use pipe-thread connections where disassembly may be required, such as at connections to valves.

Assembling a glued joint is simple and quick. File off any burrs left from cutting, then with a damp rag clean all the surfaces to be joined. Dry the surfaces, then apply primer/cleaner to clean and soften the plastic and thus enhance the bonding of the joint. Apply solvent cement to the mating surfaces, push the pieces together and give them a quarter turn to spread the cement. Wipe off squeezed-out solvent, which can weaken the pipe wall. The joint sets up almost immediately, but the manufacturers warn against applying water pressure for 24 hours. Solvent cements may not bond well when applied above or below certain temperatures, so check the instructions for yours. Since the main line is always under pressure, test it under full pressure for leaks, uncemented joints and cracks. Cut a leaky joint apart and redo it. I test sprinkler lines, too, even though small leaks there don't matter so much.

Galvanized-steel pipe is considerably more expensive and difficult to install than plastic. (Galvanized-steel pipe is often referred to as "iron pipe," a vestige of the days before steel replaced wrought iron for general plumbing.) It's more durable than plastic in exposed locations, but its internal surfaces are rougher, and over time corrosion and deposits further reduce its flow capacity. I use Teflon tape as a joint sealant instead of pipe dope, a sort of goo sold in a tube, because it's neat and effective. Cutting and threading pipe requires special equipment, so I buy all lengths to size, pre-threaded. To join plastic to galvanized steel, use a male,

plastic threaded fitting to a female, steel threaded fitting. (The other way around, the plastic can split due to internal stressing.) I've had lots of trouble with leaky plastic-to-steel joints. More Teflon and torque seems to help, but I've read cautions against using more than light pressure. Pipe dope might work better than the Teflon.

Unlike galvanized steel, copper tube can easily be cut to any length and joined with slip fittings by soldering. Copper is a little more expensive than galvanized steel, but it is lighter, has slightly smaller outside diameters and offers less flow resistance. A wheeled pipe cutter is the only suitable tool for cutting copper. Some skill is required to produce a tight, clean joint, but after a little surreptitious reading at the hardware-store bookshelf and some practice, I was getting good results.

Joining sections of copper or brass to galvanized steel can lead to corrosion at the coupling because the different electrical properties of the metals create an electrical current across the junction. Most plumbing codes require a nonmetallic insulating coupling (available at hardware stores) between the two metals to prevent any current flow. However, this is required only if both metal sections are separately grounded, as occurs, for example, when a copper pipe extension from an appliance is joined to an existing galvanized-steel water line. Because the brass end of my manifold is freestanding 8 in. above ground, it's not grounded other than by the connection to the galvanized-steel pipe, so no insulator was needed.   —D.R.

are important. Basically, it is easier to push a given volume of water through a large pipe than through a small pipe, and everything practical should be done to minimize restrictions in the system.

First, you need to find out the water flow and pressure supplied by your city service or well. Table 1 shows the total available flow from a water service according to the size of the meter (usually ⅝ in., ¾ in. or 1 in.), the size of the pipe from the meter, and the water pressure, measured when no water is being delivered (called the static pressure). To measure the pressure, make sure no water is flowing in the system, attach a pressure gauge to an outside faucet and turn the faucet on. My $10 hardware-store meter measured 80 lb. per sq. in. (psi), which is relatively high. Pressure fluctuates in city systems, so I metered again in the evening, but the results were the same. My water meter is in a concrete box set in the ground near the street. The size is often stamped on a meter; mine wasn't, so I estimated it was ¾ in., the same size as the pipe connecting it to the house. As the table shows, these factors indicate an available flow of 18.5 gal. per minute (gpm).

My house is about 50 ft. from the meter and is serviced by ¾-in. galvanized-steel pipe. It would have been easiest to tap into the exposed pipe and shutoff valve at the house. But, as shown in Table 2, a flow of 15 gpm through 50 ft. of ¾-in. steel pipe would suffer a pressure drop of about 17 lb.—some 20% of the available pressure. However, if I tapped in at a hose bib near the meter and ran 1¼-in. PVC pipe the same distance, the drop would be less than 1 lb. I decided to use 1¼-in. pipe for the entire main line, as pressure loss over a possible 300-ft. length would be less than 5 lb. (Fittings cause pressure loss, too. For ease of calculation, the loss for each is equated to that of a given length of straight pipe of the same type and diameter. For 1¼-in. pipe, these losses are small, so I didn't bother to determine them. If you need to do so, *Turf Irrigation Manual* has an excellent chart.)

I replaced the hose bib with a gate valve, then double-checked my calculations by measuring the actual wide-open flow directly. The gate valve isolates the irrigation system from domestic water lines, and its full-diameter, straight-through bore causes little pressure drop. I opened the valve fully and timed the needle on the water meter with a stopwatch while counting out five revolutions—5 cu. ft. (Clocking the time to fill a 5-gal. container would also work.) Converting cubic feet to gallons (0.134 cu. ft. in 1 gal.) and dividing by the time gave me 17.5 gpm, surprisingly close to the chart's calculated value. I found throughout the installation that, where possible, it was worth checking calculat-

TABLE 1: Available water flow

Size of water meter (in.)	Size of service line (in.)	Static water pressure (lb. / in.²)										
		30	35	40	45	50	55	60	65	70	75	80
		Gallons per minute (gpm)										
⅝	½	2.0	3.5	5.0	6.0	6.5	7.0	7.5	8.0	9.0	-	-
⅝	¾	3.5	5.0	7.0	8.5	9.5	10.0	11.0	11.5	13.0	-	-
¾	¾	6.0	7.5	9.0	10.0	12.0	13.0	14.0	15.0	16.0	17.5	18.5
¾	1	7.5	10.0	11.5	13.5	15.0	16.0	17.5	18.5	20.0	21.0	22.0
1	1	10.0	12.0	13.5	17.0	19.5	22.0	23.5	25.0	26.0	28.0	29.0
1	1¼	12.0	15.5	17.5	21.0	23.5	26.0	28.5	30.5	32.5	34.0	35.0

Note: Table assumes irrigation-system pipe to be PVC, and that system is connected to water supply no more than 50 ft. from water meter.
Data courtesy of GardenAmerica/Lawn Genie.

TABLE 2: Pressure loss (straight pipe)

Blue values—Schedule 40 PVC pipe
Black values—Schedule 40 galvanized-steel pipe

GPM	Pipe size (in.)					
	½	¾	1	1¼	1½	2
	Loss per 100 ft. (lb. / in.²)					
5	9.88 / 17.85	2.42 / 4.54	0.728 / 1.40	0.187 / 0.370	0.088 / 0.175	0.026 / 0.052
10	- / 64.35	8.72 / 16.38	2.62 / 5.06	0.676 / 1.33	0.316 / 0.629	0.092 / 0.187
15	- / -	18.46 / 34.68	5.56 / 10.71	1.43 / 2.82	0.669 / 1.33	0.196 / 0.395
20	- / -	- / 59.05	9.46 / 18.24	2.44 / 4.80	1.14 / 2.27	0.333 / 0.673
24	- / -	- / 82.74	13.26 / 25.56	3.41 / 6.73	1.60 / 3.18	0.467 / 0.943
30	- / -	- / -	- / 38.62	5.16 / 10.17	2.41 / 4.80	0.705 / 1.42

Figures from *Turf Irrigation Manual*.

ed values against actual performance.

Automatic, electrically operated valves commonly come in ¾-in. and 1-in. sizes. The larger ones have lower pressure drops for a given flow of water and can thus deliver more water. I chose 1-in. valves. (Valves can also take care of code requirements for backflow prevention. See the sidebar at the top of the facing page.) In addition, I decided that I would run my system one valve at a time, even though my timer allows me to use two at once. When two valves are open simultaneously, each delivers half or less of the available flow. This may be useful for drip, but it wouldn't suit my sprinklers.

To find out how many sprinkler heads a single valve could serve and still maintain sufficient pressure for adequate coverage, I divided a conservative 15-gpm supply by the rated flow of each sprinkler head (usually marked on the packaging). For example, my impulse sprinklers are rated at 4.4 gpm at 40 lb. pressure. Dividing 15 by 4.4 indicated that the system should handle at least three heads. But, when I tested the assembled line, I found that two was the limit. Adding the third cut the heads' coverage below what I wanted. When I tested spray heads, however, I found that a single valve could run up to ten at ample coverage. Though it

can be done by calculation, the best way to know how many sprinklers to put on a line is to assemble it and see how it works.

Knowing the coverage I could expect from each valve, I could now plan how to distribute the water around the property. There are two basic approaches to this. In the first, all the valves are installed together and all the pipes run radially from them to the areas to be watered. This is the best method for small systems.

My property is 200 ft. deep, though, and the back half is a slope crossed by stone-walled terraces, concrete paths and a large patio. A radial fan of underground pipe runs would be hard to install. I decided I could minimize pipe-laying by running a single 1¼-in. main-line pipe to the various areas of the yard, installing valve manifolds near the areas to be serviced and extending the system as needed.

Installation

The least enjoyable installation task is usually digging trenches for the pipe. Walls and terraces make most of my locations inaccessible to a power trencher, so I dig my trenches 6 in. to 8 in. deep with a narrow "sharp shooter" type of spade. It's important to make the bottom of each trench as smooth as possible, and to remove all rocks, which can damage

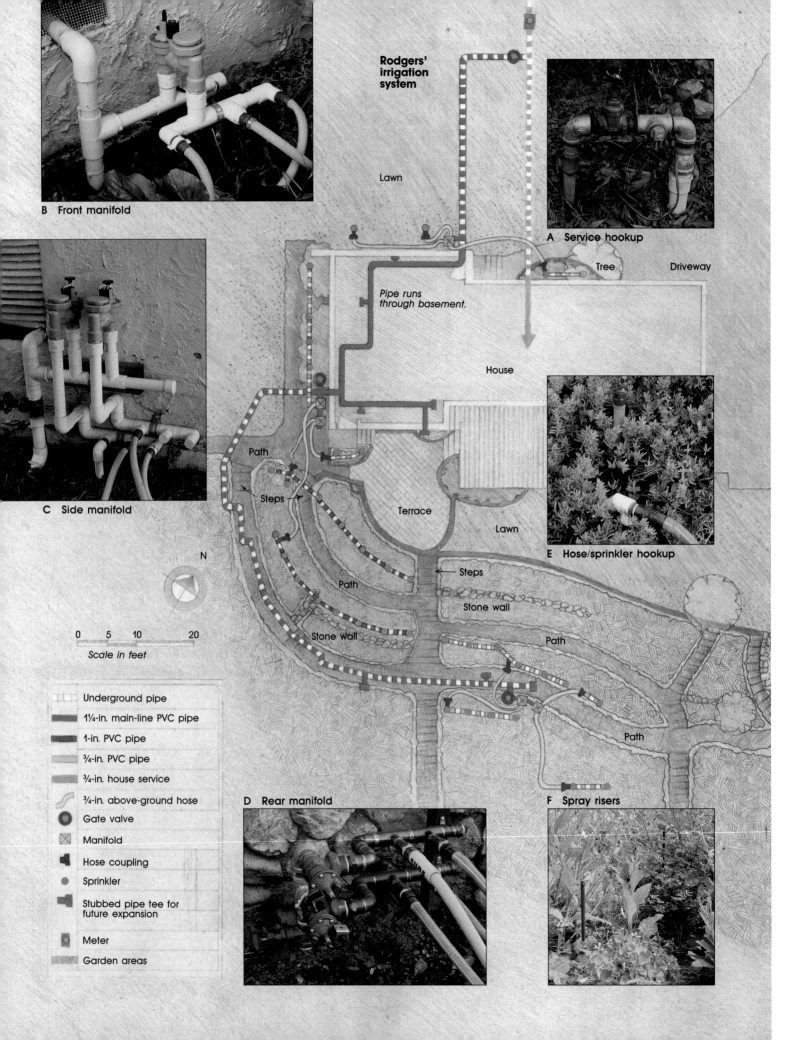

B Front manifold

Rodgers' irrigation system

Lawn

A Service hookup

C Side manifold

Pipe runs
through basement.

Tree   Driveway

House

E Hose/sprinkler hookup

Path

Steps

Terrace

Lawn

Steps

Stone wall

Path

Path

Stone wall

N

Path

0   5   10   20
Scale in feet

	Underground pipe
	1¼-in. main-line PVC pipe
	1-in. PVC pipe
	¾-in. PVC pipe
	¾-in. house service
	¾-in. above-ground hose
	Gate valve
	Manifold
	Hose coupling
	Sprinkler
	Stubbed pipe tee for future expansion
	Meter
	Garden areas

D Rear manifold

F Spray risers

PVC pipe. If your soil is very rocky, use sand or fine soil to line the bottom and cover the pipe before backfilling. In areas where the ground freezes, you needn't bury pipe deeper, but you must provide drainage to avoid frozen water in the pipes. In general, this can be done with simple drain valves and gravel sumps, installed at all low points in the system.

Lawns are hard to trench. The sod must be removed and put back or the area reseeded, and the soil is usually well packed (watering very generously for a week prior to digging can help). Where possible, I route pipe around lawn areas. Garden beds are easier to trench, but require allowances for tilling. Rather than laying pipe deep enough to till over, I simply dig up the line when tilling, an easy task for sections connected to the manifold with above-ground hose. If you're burying pipe permanently, galvanized-steel pipe will survive encounters with errant tines better than plastic will.

Tapping into the water service by replacing the old hose bib with a gate valve was fairly straightforward, as shown in photo **A** on the facing page. If you need to cut into the existing service and install a tee fitting, I suggest having a plumber do this work. After laying 50 ft. of 1¼-in. PVC main line to the house, I ran the pipe up the wall and through a ventilation grill into the crawlway under the house. The first valve manifold (photo **B**) comes off the line just before the grill, and its three outlets service the front yard.

From the grill, I ran the main pipe under the house, attaching it to the walls with pipe hangers, and out a grill at the back. I installed several plugged pipe tees along the way for future expansion. I chose this route instead of trenching around the house because it avoided tunneling through the rocky underpinnings of several concrete slabs.

I installed the second manifold near the back vent (photo **C** and drawing at right). Its two valves serve side and back sections of the yard. From here the main line descends the slope in back, a fairly tortuous route due to the terrace walls and paths. Frustrated by the limitations of 45° and 90° elbows, I found that a 20-ft. section of 1¼-in. PVC pipe can be bent 20° to 25°, while 20 ft. of ¾-in. pipe can be redirected almost a full 90°. At selected spots, I installed pipe tees in the line and attached short sections of pipe with caps at the end for future expansion.

My third manifold (photo **D**) is metal rather than plastic. I tapped into the main line with plastic fittings, then switched to galvanized steel. I could have used plastic for the underground section, but the manifold is in a high-traffic area and the steel pipe helps insulate the plastic main line from shock in the event of a blow to the exposed manifold. The 1-in. automatic

valves are brass, the outlets copper. Unlike the plastic valves in the other manifolds, these don't have built-in anti-siphon devices, as I had installed a system-wide backflow preventer by this time.

In several areas I've connected valves directly to sprinkler heads with underground pipe, using 1-in. pipe for long lines and in those requiring full flow, and ¾-in. pipe for short or limited-flow sections. For most sections, though, I dug in a pipe fitted with one or more sprinkler heads and an above-ground female hose-connector adapter (photo **E**). Between this adapter and the valve outlet, I run ¾-in. garden hose, cut to length. By running hose over tough terrain, I saved considerable effort in pipe-laying and gained a lot of flexibility. Eventually I'll replace many of the hoses with underground pipe, but not until I'm happy with the sprinkler type and placement I've tested out with the hose setup.

Sprinkler placement on a line is determined by the type of head and the coverage you want. I usually put spray heads 5 ft. apart, which also makes for the most efficient use of the 20-ft. lengths

of pipe I get at the hardware store. For flower beds and borders, I use ½-in. PVC risers threaded on both ends, available in lengths from 2 in. to 48 in. One end fits a threaded reducing tee glued into the underground line; the other end fits a brass spray head (photo **F**). Teflon joint tape minimizes leakages and makes it much easier to undo a joint when I need to increase the riser length as plants grow. Be very careful when placing plants in relation to sprinkler heads—irises, for example, make a very effective water screen. I installed impulse-type sprinklers in the borders of my lawn areas, to avoid trenching the lawn for the recessed pop-up sprinklers often used to allow mowing.

In two years, I've installed only part of the complete system I envision, but it has had a major impact on my gardening activities. New additions will take years. If I did not enjoy the work, I would have given up in frustration long ago. But I guess that sums up gardening in general. □

Dave Rodgers manages a radioactivity testing lab when he isn't gardening.

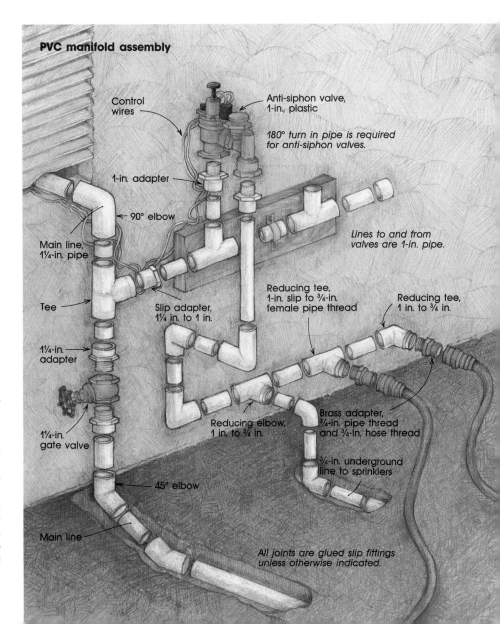

PVC manifold assembly

Control wires

Anti-siphon valve, 1-in., plastic

180° turn in pipe is required for anti-siphon valves.

1-in. adapter

90° elbow

Main line, 1¼-in. pipe

Lines to and from valves are 1-in. pipe.

Tee

Slip adapter, 1¼ in. to 1 in.

Reducing tee, 1-in. slip to ¾-in. female pipe thread

Reducing tee, 1 in. to ¾ in.

1¼-in. adapter

1¼-in. gate valve

Reducing elbow, 1 in. to ¾ in.

Brass adapter, ¾-in. pipe thread and ¾-in. hose thread

¾-in. underground line to sprinklers

45° elbow

Main line

All joints are glued slip fittings unless otherwise indicated.

Photos: Dave Rodgers; drawings: Laura B. Goodwin

A collection of pots, cellpacks and mini flats shows the diversity of seed-starting gear available to gardeners. You have to balance cost, durability and convenience to decide what equipment suits the way you start seeds.

Seed-Starting Gear
How to choose the right equipment for your needs

by Chris Curless

My wife is a seed-starting widow. When I set out last year to try all the seed-starting gear I could find,

she groaned: another winter without a husband. But I was excited. After years of starting seeds in the same old containers, I could try the tantalizing gear offered in catalogs and garden centers.

My aim was to get a firsthand feel for the features, construction and capabilities of every seed-starting product

that gardeners are likely to meet. I found that there are three main types: flats, pots and cellpacks. These various containers differ largely in their size, ease of use and practicality. Each type has its advantages and disadvantages. I hope to tell you enough about them so you can decide which ones best match your needs.

Photo: Robert Marsala

Lots of seeds, one container

Flats are shallow, rectangular containers, usually made of black plastic, with solid sides and a grid bottom. They can accommodate hundreds of seeds. You can also make your own flats out of thin strips of wood, with a slatted bottom for drainage.

Flats are excellent for starting large numbers of seeds. They come in a variety of sizes, but 10 in. × 20 in. and 11 in. × 22 in. are the most commonly used sizes. Most gardeners who use flats sow the seeds in rows and then transplant the strongest seedlings into individual containers.

For gardeners who have only limited growing space, the chief drawback of flats is their size. It's possible to start more than one kind of seed in a flat, but unless the seedlings germinate and grow at approximately the same rate, you have to uproot one block of seedlings for transplanting while trying to leave the rest undisturbed.

As an alternative to large flats, I use mini flats, usually called garden packs or market packs. They're made

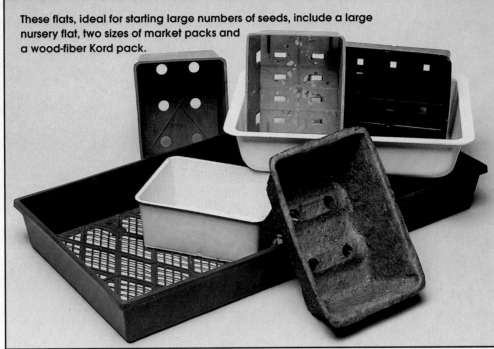

These flats, ideal for starting large numbers of seeds, include a large nursery flat, two sizes of market packs and a wood-fiber Kord pack.

of heavy-duty plastic and measure about 5 in. × 6 in. or 5 in. × 7 in. You probably won't find plastic market packs for sale; I get mine from garden centers, which sometimes sell seedlings in them. You may also run across pressed wood-fiber packs called Kord packs. They have similar dimensions and they're just as durable as their plastic counterparts.

A variety of squares and rounds

Pots can be circular or square (square pots use growing space more efficiently) and they come in a large variety of sizes, from 2¼ in. (measured across the top of the pot) to 6 in. and up. I find 3-in. or 4-in. pots to be ideal for seed-starting and transplanting. They're large enough to hold several seeds or seedlings, but they don't take up much space.

Pots have several advantages. They're useful for starting one or two seeds of vigorous growers such as beans or morning-glories. These plants come on so strong that it makes no sense to sow them in a flat and then transplant them to a pot. Pots are also excellent for starting a small group of seeds. Rather than sow one large flat with an entire packet of seeds, I prefer to start different kinds of seeds in their own small pots—one or two dozen seeds per pot, depending on the size of the seeds. With different seeds in separate pots, I don't have to worry about varying germination rates. When a set

These pots, for starting one to a dozen seeds, are made of terra cotta, plastic, peat, newspaper or milk cartons. The tool at the right makes soil blocks.

of seedlings is up and growing, I transplant the seedlings into cell packs or pots of their own.

The variety of pots is enormous. Those sold through catalogs or at garden centers are usually made of terra cotta, plastic or peat. Because terra cotta pots readily allow air and moisture to pass through them, the soil mix they contain dries out faster

than soil mix in plastic pots. This permeability makes for extra watering and increases the chances that a few days of inattention will result in dessicated seedlings.

Pots made of peat are also widely available. Standard peat pots have the look and feel of lightweight, textured cardboard. Circular or square, they come in 2¼-in., 3-in. or 4-in.

Photos: Susan Kahn

sizes. They also come attached in double rows of smaller, square pots.

A variation on the peat pot is the peat pellet, a disc of compressed peat. Once saturated with water, it expands into a small, barrel-shaped pot about 2 in. tall and wide, held together with a fine plastic netting.

Whatever their shape or their size, peat pots are intended to be planted with the seedling, so there's no need to disturb the roots. The roots will grow through the peat into the surrounding soil. (When planting peat pots, take care to remove any portion of the peat that protrudes above soil level. The peat can wick moisture away from the soil mix and cause it to dry out even though the surrounding soil is moist.)

Peat pots have their drawbacks. Like terra cotta pots, they dry out quickly. Drying can be a big problem when hardening off seedlings (acclimating them to life outdoors), particularly on sunny or windy days. Peat pots are also more expensive than other pots in the long run because you plant them along with the seedlings.

The author separates two seedlings started in a pot for transplanting to a six-pack. Starting seeds in a pot makes it possible to sow only what you need and then pick the best seedlings to transplant individually into cellpacks or pots.

You can also buy pots made out of paper. The pots are glued together in a honeycomb and come with a corrugated plastic carrying tray. You can make your own pots out of newspaper with a simple wooden press called a Potmaker. Pots made of paper share many of the pros and cons of peat pots.

You can also recycle household refuse for starting seeds. With a few holes punched for drainage, recycled containers, such as milk cartons, tin cans and plastic tubs, work just fine. They're generally are not very durable, but you've already paid for them.

I'll describe soil blocks here, though they're not really pots. Blocks of compressed soil mix, they serve as pots without walls. Soil blocks are made with a strange-looking tool that compresses moist soil mix into cubes. Sow seeds by pressing them into the tops of the cubes. At planting time, the seedling goes into the ground block and all. Although tools that make 2-in. blocks are the most readily available, you can also find block-makers that stamp out ¾-in. and 4-in. blocks. Because soil blocks must be kept in trays and must be well separated from one another (to prevent roots from growing into neighboring blocks), they may not be practical for gardeners who are short on space.

Many little cells for seedlings

Cellpacks are clusters of small pots attached together as a unit. The most familiar cellpacks are the six-packs that line up in front of garden centers in spring, full of marigold and tomato seedlings. Cellpacks are made either of thin green or black plastic or of thicker white polystyrene. The size and shape of the cells varies from 1-in. square, 3-in. deep cells to rectangular cells 2½ in. × 2 in. × 2 in. The number of cells per unit ranges from 3 to as many as 200 or more.

Cellpacks have several advantages. They conserve space by grouping small pots tightly together. They also make transporting seedlings more convenient; one six pack is much easier to carry around than six tiny pots. And because the root systems of the seedlings are kept separate, you can remove a seedling from its cell without having to tear it free from its neighbors.

You can sow seeds directly into cellpacks or transplant seedlings into them. The directions that came with all the cellpacks I tried suggested planting one or two seeds per cell. This is fine if you're starting seeds that are very likely to germinate. But with old seeds, or seeds with special needs, you can end up with lots of empty

Plastic cellpacks sit atop a thick-walled polystyrene unit with 128 cells. The cells keep seedlings separate.

cells. I collect a lot of my own seeds, often from plants that I've never before tried to start from seeds. Unless I find tips in a book, I have no idea what conditions the seeds require to germinate. For me it makes sense to start most of my seeds in small pots or market packs and then transplant the seedlings into cellpacks before setting them out in the garden. If a group of seeds fails to germinate, I haven't lost much space to the experiment.

Photos: top, Robert Marsala; bottom, Susan Kahn

Watering aids

In your perusal of gardening catalogs and garden center shelves, you're likely to run across seed-starting accessories—watering trays, clear plastic domes and perhaps capillary matting, all of which are designed to simplify watering. Sometimes one or more of these items are sold with flats or cellpacks as a package; they're usually available separately, also.

Watering trays, which look like plastic flats without drainage holes, are for bottom-watering containers of seedlings. Bottom-watering makes sense for indoor seed-starting because it eliminates splashing. It also ensures that you are wetting the soil mix in your containers evenly; it's easy to miss a cell in a cellpack or to fail to saturate it when watering from above. To bottom-water, fill a watering tray with water (with a dash of liquid fertilizer) and set the containers into it. The soil mix in the containers will soak up the water through the drain holes. When the soil mix becomes saturated (which may take a few minutes), remove the containers. Then pour the excess water from the tray.

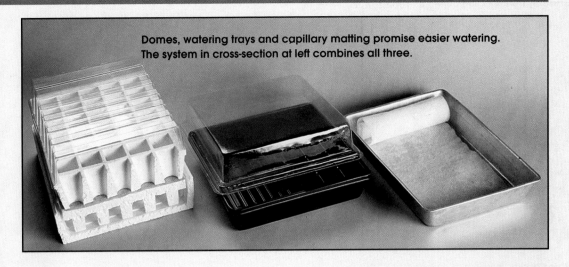

Domes, watering trays and capillary matting promise easier watering. The system in cross-section at left combines all three.

Clear plastic domes are supposed to help keep the soil mix moist and the humidity high while seeds are germinating. Some gardeners swear by them, but I'm not convinced they make a significant difference unless your soil mix dries out very rapidly. Once the seedlings have emerged, remove the dome—the same humidity that encouraged the seeds to germinate now favors the growth of the damping-off fungus, which topples and kills young seedlings.

For forgetful or especially busy gardeners, capillary matting allows containers to water themselves for long periods of time. Capillary matting is a lightly woven fabric that draws water from a pool and delivers it, against gravity, to the bottoms of containers, which draw the water up through the drain holes. You can purchase matting separately and design your own set-up, or you can purchase a ready-made unit called the Accelerated Propagation System (APS). A block of polystyrene cells sits on a piece of capillary matting. The capillary matting rests, in turn, on a polystyrene platform, which stands on stilts in a tray of water. If you use lights, you'll need room overhead, since the system stands 7 in. tall. My unit worked fine for two crops of seedlings.

What to buy?

Assess your needs before you buy seed-starting gear. How many seeds do you plan to start? How much time do you have? Seedlings must be coddled until they finally become established in the garden (a process that takes weeks and sometimes months). If your needs are small and your time is short, consider buying a package that includes a set of cellpacks, a watering tray, and perhaps a dome. Or buy a system with capillary matting. You'll pay more for the gear, but you'll have to water less frequently. If you plan to start large numbers of seeds or have plenty of time to watch and water seedlings, you'll do fine by sowing and transplanting in flats, pots or cellpacks.

Compared to buying plants, seed-starting is relatively inexpensive (unless you add in the value of your time), but it pays to shop around for seed-starting gear. You'll pay extra for convenient packages and for brand names. In addition to the up-front cost, consider durability. Paper and peat pots, soil blocks and recycled milk cartons last for just one use. Many cellpacks are made of paper-thin plastic and can be cleaned and reused for only one or two seasons. The sturdier flats, market packs and pots will last for years. Equipment that will do the job season after season may be worth the extra initial expense.

It's also possible to start seeds without opening your wallet. I've started seeds in used plastic pots and market packs. When the seedlings have a couple of sets of true leaves, I transplant them into recycled nursery cellpacks. Rather than purchase watering trays, I bottom water my seedlings in an aluminum oven pan, grudgingly loaned to me by my wife.

Every gardener I talk to uses a slightly different set of techniques to start seeds. Whatever equipment you use, you'll still get a thrill from seeing your tiny charges nudge through the soil and reach for the light. ☐

Chris Curless is an assistant editor at Fine Gardening.

SOURCES

Most garden centers and hardware stores carry a variety of seed-starting equipment. Many seed catalogs and garden-supply catalogs offer a similar variety. The mail-order companies below carry equipment described by the author.

W. Atlee Burpee & Co., Warminster, PA 18974, 800-888-1447. Catalog free. Kord fiber packs and Potmaker.

Gardener's Supply Company, 128 Intervale Road, Burlington, VT 05401, 800-863-1700. Catalog free. APS, capillary matting and paper pots.

Harmony Farm Supply and Nursery, P.O. Box 460, Graton, CA 95444, 707-823-9125. Catalog $2. Soil-block makers.

A Pot for any Plant
Clay and plastic offer choices

Unglazed clay pots have an earthy, enduring beauty. With care, they will last indefinitely. They range in height from small to large, and some have decorative designs as well.

by Delilah Smittle

Clay and plastic pots are so basic to gardening and so abundantly available that they are often taken for granted. But there are variations in pot styles and materials that can affect the health of your plants. If you know what features to look for when shopping for a quality pot, you will get many years of service from it. You'll also be most satisfied with your pot if you know how to match its size, shape and material to the needs of your plant.

I've been a keen collector of clay and plastic pots for as long as I can remember. My most intense period of potting was during the ten years that I owned a home greenhouse. Each spring I started seeds and hardened off young plants in pots. I progressed

through each growing season, planting patio-sized pots and festooning the eaves of the house and garage with hanging baskets. In winter I potted up tropical plants and cuttings. I've purchased new clay and plastic pots from garden centers and discount stores. I've experimented with pots shaped like rabbits, frogs and sea shells that I bought in import stores. I've even scoured garage sales for worn, but serviceable, pots. Here's the information on basic clay and plastic pots that I have unearthed over more than a decade of experimentation.

Like many products that are made to last, pots don't have to be new to be good. Knowing how to store and clean pots properly will enable you to keep them from fading, cracking or breaking for many years. And, if you know how to properly clean pots before reusing them, you can protect your plants from disease (see "Disinfecting and cleaning pots" on p. 63.)

Characteristics of clay and plastic pots

Clay pots—Unglazed clay, or terracotta, pots are actually made of a type of soil and are fired in kilns, or ovens, during manufacturing (terracotta means "baked earth"). Because clay pots provide a home for plant roots that nearly duplicates the conditions roots have when they grow in the ground, clay pots are considered safe for plants and for the environment. (Clay or plastic, the pots best suited for growing plants have drainage holes in the bottom.)

Being a traditionalist, I like the texture, warm color and heft of clay pots, and I prefer them for potting plants for a number of reasons. Pots made of clay provide a healthy home for the roots of many plants. Their thick walls protect roots from rapid changes in temperature. The porosity of the clay allows air and moisture to penetrate the sides of the pot where it can be

Plastic pots come in many shapes, sizes and colors, and with proper care can last for ten years or more. Fiberglass pots, such as the gray, basket-weave pot shown here, are made of plastic reinforced with glass fibers.

taken up by fine roots that grow along pot walls. Because clay is porous and the walls of clay pots wick excess moisture from the potting medium, they are ideal for plants that require good drainage and dry soil. These characteristics also make clay pots a good choice for gardeners like me, who have a tendency to overwater.

I've learned through experience, however, that clay pots can dry out too quickly for sprouting seeds or for moisture-loving plants. I may be traditional in taste and love clay pots for their beauty, but I am also practical, so I favor plastic pots for keeping the growing medium moist enough to germinate seeds and to keep the roots of ferns and moisture-loving tropical plants healthy.

What about that crusty white film on the outside of clay pots? It is formed when mineral salts dissolved in water are wicked from the potting medium through the walls of the pots. I find pot walls that are mottled with these salts picturesque, but some gardeners find them unsightly. If you do, you can scrub the salts off.

Plastic pots—Plastic pots are flexible and strong and have the additional benefit of weighing less than their clay counterparts. And if you crave color more than I do, plastic pots can supply it—they come in basic black, white and earth tones, plus many designer colors. Unlike the porous walls of clay pots, the walls of plastic pots do not allow water to escape, making them a good choice for moisture-loving plants and gardeners who don't water frequently. If you're growing plants that require especially good drainage or dry soil and you still want to use plastic pots, fill them with a fast-draining potting mix.

The materials plastic pots are made of are considered inert and safe for growing plants. And some plastic pots have the environmental benefit of being made of a type of plastic that is suitable for recycling when the pots are no longer usable. (All unglazed clay pots are recyclable, too.)

In my experience, the durability, and therefore the cost, of a plastic pot depends on its construction—both increase with thickness. Plastic pots range in sturdiness from nearly paper-thin, dispensable pots to heavy-duty, utilitarian pots. I've had thin plastic pots last for only one day of careless handling, although a few have survived for five years with less vigorous usage. If plastic pots have thicker walls, they are

This symbol (a triangle formed by three arrows), when molded into a plastic pot, indicates that the pot can be recycled.

generally better. With ordinary care, these pots can withstand repeated use for over ten years.

However, the walls of most plastic pots are thinner than those of clay pots and offer little insulation for roots. Black plastic especially can actually act as a solar collector, heating the potting medium to temperatures that can damage roots. If you notice plants in plastic pots wilting, move them into the shade.

Sunlight is hard on plastic pots. It can make them fade, get brittle and break easily. Many plastic pots are treated with ultraviolet light inhibitors, however, which reduce fading and maintain flexibility. These pots are not always labeled as ultraviolet-protected, but if labels recommend using pots outdoors, they probably have this protection.

Pot shapes

Basic clay and plastic pots share simple shapes. Most pots have round or straight sides that narrow from top to bottom. The tops usually have a thickened or raised edge called a lip, or shoulder, that is designed to be strong enough to support a pot filled with heavy, moist soil when you pick it up. Clay is heavy and hard to mold, so mass-produced clay pots are most available, and most affordable, in small to medium sizes (see photo on p. 60).

Plastic pots, which are easy to manufacture, come in a wide range of sizes—from small to very large—and shapes—rectangular, square, or round-walled (see photo on p. 61). Mass-produced small, medium and large plastic pots are available at discount stores and garden centers.

Square, straight-sided pots are usually small to medium in size and are most available in plastic, because clay can't be easily molded into this shape. I like small, square plastic pots for starting seeds and young plants because they line up neatly on my growing bench and hold more growing medium than round pots of the same size.

Pots come in many sizes

Pots are sized according to the inside diameter or width of the top of the pot and are graduated in size, usually in 1 in. increments. Small and medium-sized American-made clay pots are widely available at discount stores and garden centers; they begin at 1½ in. diameter pots called thumb pots, and graduate in diameter to 2 in., 2¼ in., 2½ in., 3 in. and then upwards in 1 in. increments to 16 in. Clay pots larger than 16 in., which are difficult to mass-produce, are usually imported and are less plentiful. Plastic pots, which are made in the United States, are available in a wide range of standard sizes beginning at 4 in. in diameter and increasing in 1-in. increments to 20 in.

Three basic proportions characterize most pots. The most-used, which is

The pot at the bottom of this stack is well-used and covered with mineral deposits, but its exterior is intact and strong. The top pot is new, but the white flecks in its sides are flaws—lime deposits that absorb moisture and expand, causing pitting and crumbling, as shown in the middle pot.

called a standard, is as deep as it is wide at the shoulder. So, a 6-in. standard pot is 6 in. tall and 6 in. in diameter at the shoulder. Standard pots are suited to many plants. The tall shape visually balances vertically-shaped plants and is ideal for plants that don't have spreading root systems. Shallower pots are designed for plants with spreading root systems. A pot that is slightly shorter than a standard is called a three-quarter pot or an azalea pot. As its name indicates, the three-quarter pot is 75% as high as it is wide. For example, a 6-in. three-quarter pot is 4½ in. tall and 6 in. in diameter. This type of pot is my favorite because its squatty shape makes it hard to tip over, and yet it is deep enough for the root systems of many plants. The pots for bulbs, called pans, are even more shallow—only half as tall as they are wide. A 6 in. bulb pan is only 3 in. deep and 6 in. in diameter. Bulb pans are not just for bulbs—they are ideal for plants that spread by runners because they provide more soil surface than standard pots of the same volume.

When sizing a pot to a particular plant, look for one that is big enough to allow room for the roots to grow, but small enough so that the roots can absorb all the moisture from the potting medium between waterings. If the pot is too big, the soil may remain constantly soggy, inviting root rot or fungal disease. Conventional wisdom advises choosing a pot that is 1 in. or 2 in. wider than the widest part of the plant's root system (use roomier pots only for fast growers). Repot plants into pots 1-in. or 2-in. larger when most of their roots have reached the pot walls. (You can unpot plants once or twice a year to check root growth; simply repot in the same pot if roots haven't reached the walls.)

Recognizing quality

One clay or plastic pot may look and cost much the same as another of that material, but there are ways to evaluate quality.

Clay pots—Clay pots are susceptible to cracking, so before buying one, make sure it's sound. Hold the pot up by hooking a finger through the drain hole and tap it on the shoulder. A good clay pot will ring like a bell; cracked pots will sound flat or dull. If the pot doesn't ring, don't buy it.

Pots that are baked in kilns derive much of their strength from how they're fired. As time and temperature increase, the minerals within the clay harden, or vitrify. American and European pots are reliably durable, but some imported pots are fired at lower temperatures or for shorter periods of time, and can vary in durability. As mineral salts leach through, the walls of inferior pots gradually flake and crumble. It is easy to detect weak pots—they are so soft that you can scratch them with your fingernail.

The purity of clay used in pots also affects their durability. All clay contains lime impurities. When quality pots are made, the lime is filtered out of the clay before manufacturing. But lime deposits can remain throughout the clay of an inferior pot (some will be visible on the surface as white, gritty spots). Since lime particles are more absorbent than clay, they can swell when moist, creating blisters that will burst, causing the surface of the pot to flake. If you spot lime deposits in a pot, pass it by (see photo on the facing page).

Clay that contains sand can be made into durable pots if it is fired at high temperatures; these pots become dense and ceramic-like. But if clay that contains sand is fired at low temperatures, the resulting pot can crumble away over time. You can spot these pots because their surface will actually have a sandy texture.

Plastic pots—Plastic pots, too, can vary in quality. Thickness and flexibility of pot walls are indications that a plastic pot is made to last. The pot walls should look thick enough to support the weight of the wet soil that they will hold—the bigger the pot, the thicker the walls should be. To check flexibility, squeeze the pot; plastic pots should be resilient enough to withstand being bumped or dropped without breaking.

There is only one exception to this rule. Fiberglass pots are made of a plastic that is reinforced with glass fibers. Fiberglass pots are typically lightweight, thin-walled and not particularly flexible, but they are very strong and weather-resistant. It is the glass fibers, not the thickness of the plastic, that gives these pots their strength. If you look closely at the interior of a fiberglass pot, which is usually not finished as smoothly as the exterior, you may see the glass fibers embedded in the plastic. Fiberglass pots can come in many shapes and colors, but they are most often custom-made for commercial installations and are very costly. One retail mail-order catalog (Gardeners Eden, P.O. Box 7307, San Francisco, CA 94120-7307), sells fiberglass pots suitable for home gardeners in sizes ranging from 15-in. in diameter to 28 in. in diameter for prices beginning at $130. ☐

Delilah Smittle is an assistant editor at Fine Gardening *and has grown plants in pots for two decades.*

Disinfecting and cleaning pots

Pots can be reused indefinitely, but with each use, they accumulate mineral deposits and other debris inside and out that can harbor disease. So for the plant's sake, you should clean and disinfect your old pots each time you plant in them.

Mineral salts can be unsightly and can damage plants. Minerals, which are dissolved in water, leach through the walls of clay pots, forming a white film on them. They can also accumulate around the rims of both clay and plastic pots. This white, crusty film is merely unsightly when deposited on pot walls, but when it encrusts the rim of a pot, the mineral salts can dehydrate plant stems that rest there.

First disinfect, then scrub used pots. To disinfect clay pots, soak them in a solution of 1 part household bleach to 9 parts of water for ten minutes or more. Next, dip them into a solution of water and dish detergent.

Lift the pots from the soapy water and scrub away as much of the dirt and mineral deposits as you can, inside and out, using steel wool or a wire-bristle brush. Scrape any remaining mineral deposits from the pot walls and the rim of the pot with a knife. When clay pots are clean, rinse them off and soak them in a bucket of clean water until you are ready to use them. (Dry clay pots can wick moisture from the potting medium, dehydrating newly potted plants.)

Plastic pots can be disinfected and cleaned in the same way as clay pots are, except that you can easily remove salts and debris with a scouring pad. If any mineral salts cling to the rim of a plastic pot after it's been scrubbed, simply scrape them off with a knife and smooth the pot edges with steel wool. Rinse the pot clean, and it's ready to use.

—D.S.

Labels and Markers

Keep track of your plants

Editor's note: *Garden labels and markers are insurance. You may know every plant in the garden today, but eventually memory fails. If you put out three promising daylilies one spring and by fall can't remember the name of the best-flowering cultivar, forgetting hurts.*

Since everyone profits from sharing experiences, in FG #4 we asked you to tell us about your favorite labels and markers. Four readers presented especially useful ideas for homemade ones. Their letters are printed here. Readers had little to say about manufactured labels and markers, so associate editor Mark Kane did some investigating. His thoughts precede the letters. (The labels and markers he found are listed in the sources on the facing page and shown in part on pp. 64-66) Our thanks to all who wrote to us.

Mark Kane

Because so few readers wrote to us about manufactured labels and markers, I ordered every brand I could from mail-order sources that cater to gardeners. The range surprised me. Labels, which are generally looped or wired around a stem or branch, come in self-tying versions made of metal or plastic, and in wire-tied versions made of metal, plastic or wood. Markers, which are either stakes, or stanchions bearing nameplates, come in wood, plastic and metal versions, in a variety of styles and sizes.

After looking at a lot of labels and markers, I'm skeptical about the common complaint that they cost too much. Prices cluster in a middle range that struck me as reasonable. For example, excluding shipping, you can buy self-tying aluminum labels at $8 per hundred, and steel-stanchioned markers with zinc nameplates at less than $10 per hundred. Some products are downright bargains—excluding shipping, 4-in. plastic or wooden stake-style markers cost about $2.50 per hundred.

I'm also skeptical about complaints that labels and markers wear out too fast. You can find longevity. There are self-tying labels of sturdy aluminum, and markers of zinc and galvanized steel. There are two brands of aluminum labels on which you impress letters with a hard writing instrument, such as a ball-point pen. The lettering is as permanent as the metal—certainly long-lived enough for most uses. Several other brands offer thicker aluminum or zinc labels and nameplates, on which you write with a so-called permanent marking pen, an ordinary #2 pencil, a wax crayon or a grease pencil. From what I hear, the results vary. (I welcome comments from readers with experience.) Depending on conditions, writing made with a marking pen or a grease pencil lasts one to six years. But if you renew the names regularly, you have permanence. Pencil writing may last seven years or more, long enough to make renewing no chore at all. However, lettering in pencil is thinner and harder to dis-

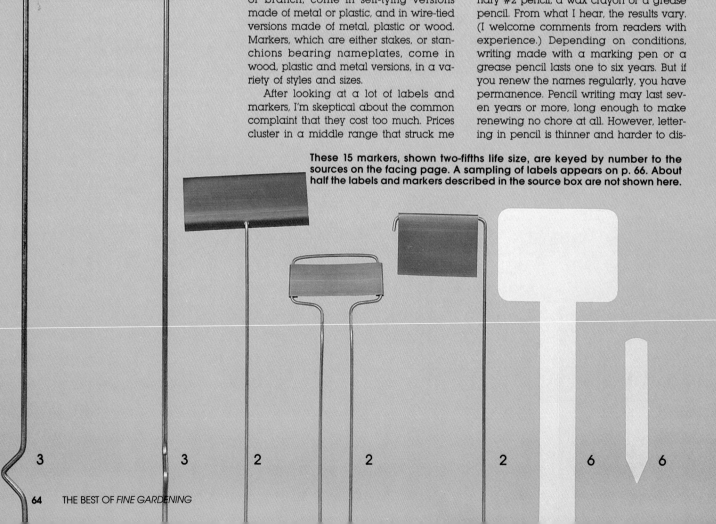

These 15 markers, shown two-fifths life size, are keyed by number to the sources on the facing page. A sampling of labels appears on p. 66. About half the labels and markers described in the source box are not shown here.

3   3   2   2   2   6   6

tinguish than lettering in marking pen, wax crayon or grease pencil.

Short-lived labels and markers have their uses. When you start trees and shrubs that might not tolerate your growing conditions, or please your taste, it makes sense to use an inexpensive wooden or plastic label the first year or two. If you start a lot of plants from seed, why not use cheaper markers in your cell-packs and flats? The markers might cost 3¢ apiece, and they don't have to last. If you need to keep track of certain annuals—three tomato varieties, for instance, or three zinnia cultivars—you can move the markers to the garden when you transplant your seedlings and expect them to last for the growing season. For perennials, you can use short-lived markers the first year or two, when the plants are on probation. Once you know which plants you'll keep, switch to longer-lived markers.

Peter Ruh

I'm semiretired after 35 years in the nursery business, and now grow only shade-tolerant perennials, including a study collection of more than 950 different hosta varieties, possibly the largest in the United States. Many hostas are very much alike. Without a fairly permanent way of labeling them, my collection would soon become a hopelessly mixed-up mess.

Over the years, I've tried a lot of labels

SOURCES

1. Amekron Products, 24232 Avenue 200, Strathmore, CA 93267. Two wire-tie labels made of sheet aluminum sandwiched around thin cardboard. Ordinary ball-point pen impresses permanent letters in the aluminum. 1-in. by 3-in. labels are $8.50 per hundred, plus shipping and handling. Sample, brochure and price list free.

2. Eon Industries, 315 Dodge St., Swanton, OH 43558. Markers with galvanized 13-ga. wire stanchions and sheet-zinc nameplates in four styles and several heights; marking pens and grease pencil. Markers range from $15.90 to $26.90 per hundred, plus shipping and handling. Brochure free.

3. Evergreen Garden Plant Labels, P.O. Box 922, Cloverdale, CA 95425. Markers in three heights with 8-ga. galvanized-steel stanchions soldered to galvanized-steel nameplates, and optional clip-on green aluminum nameplates; 8-ga. galvanized-steel stakes in two heights with double-eye tops to hold wired and self-tying labels. Markers are 75¢ each for 13-in.-tall version, optional clip-on nameplates are 25¢ each, and double-eye stakes are $7.80 per dozen for 19-in.-tall version, plus shipping and handling. Send 1st-class stamp for brochure.

4. Harlane Company, 266 Orangeburgh Rd., Old Tappan, NJ 07675. Plastic stakes and removable plastic nameplates. $26.00 per hundred, plus shipping and handling; smaller quantities available. Brochure free.

5. Mellinger's, 2326 W. South Range Rd., North Lima, OH 44452. General garden supplier carries wooden, plastic and metal markers; wire-tie wooden labels, self-tying plastic labels, and two impressible aluminum labels; marking pens and pencils. Prices range from $2.30 per

hundred for 4-in.-tall wooden markers to $10.85 per hundred for metal markers, plus shipping and handling. Catalog free.

6. Pat's Mini-Pack Labels, 785 White Rd., Watsonville, CA 95076. Label with nylon tie, self-tying strap label, and six stake-style markers. Vinyl in yellow or white. Prices include marking pen, shipping and handling; the range is $11.25 per hundred for 4-in. pot labels to $29.25 per hundred for 9½-in.-tall T-stakes with 3⅜-in. by 2½-in. nameplates. Send SASE for brochure.

7. Paw Paw Everlast Label Company, P.O. Box 93-C, Paw Paw, MI 49079. Wire-tied and self-tied etched sheet-zinc labels; eight markers with a variety of galvanized 13-ga. wire stanchions with etched sheet-zinc nameplates; three marking products. Postpaid prices range from $6.55 per hundred for 4-in.-long labels to $27.50 per hundred for 21-in.-tall markers. Brochure free.

8. S&D Enterprises, 1280 Quince Dr., Junction City, OR 97448. Self-tying aluminum labels and aluminum "mini-tags" that double as markers. Letter with #2 pencil. Labels are $8 per hundred, and mini-tags are $22 per thousand, postpaid. Send SASE for samples.

9. S-W Supply Co., P.O. Box 275, Girard, KS 66743. Three markers, two with impressible aluminum inserts, in 15-in. and 20-in. heights, with galvanized-steel stanchions and nameplates. Prices are $25.00 per hundred to $30.00 per hundred, plus shipping and handling. Brochure free.

10. Jeff and Amber Shook, P.O. Box 2, Villa Grove, CO 81155. Markers with ceramic nameplates and wooden stanchions. Nameplates also available with names of 54 vegetables, herbs and flowers. Prices range from $1.34 to $1.95 per marker. Price list and information free.

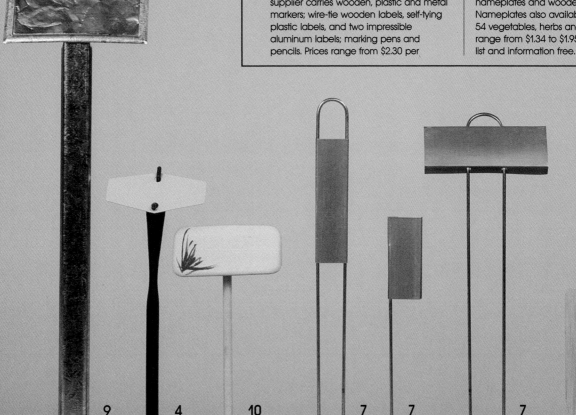

9   4   10   7   7   7   5   5

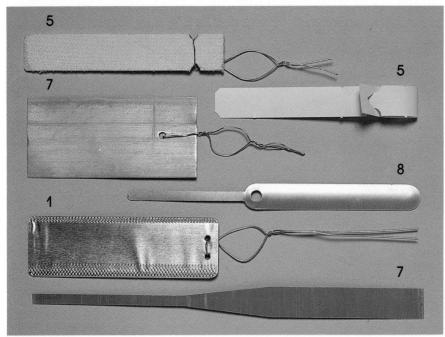

The manufactured labels shown here, which you loop or tie around stems and twigs, are keyed by number to the sources on p. 61. You letter these labels with pencil, crayon or marker, except for label 1, made of aluminum that is impressible with a ball-point pen.

and markers. The least permanent are plastic. I don't recommend them for long-term use—in time they all fade, crack and break. Unfortunately, the most permanent are too expensive for gardeners. We use a $3,000 machine to emboss raised letters on aluminum tags. (Many years ago, I met a hosta collector who made equally good tags using scrap aluminum and steel dies, but striking each letter and number by hand took a lot of time.)

I've found moderately priced alternatives to machine embossing. One comes from the S-W Supply Co. (see Sources). It consists of a metal stake with a tilted holder on top and an aluminum blank. You write on the blank with a dull pencil or an old ball-point pen, making permanently impressed letters, and then slip it into the holder. These cost about $25 per hundred. The stakes will rust in the ground, so we paint them.

For quick labels, we use tags made of thin cardboard sandwiched by two sheets of thin aluminum. You write on the aluminum, making depressed letters. Ours come from Amekron Products (see Sources), and have a wire for fastening around the plant or a stake. I have some now that are going on six years and holding up fine.

We also fashion our own stakes from redwood lath or metal, and fasten embossed or Amekron labels to them. For metal stakes, we start with stout (6-ga. or 8-ga.) galvanized wire. I get a lot of mine by salvaging the bails on 5-gal. plastic buckets. We bend one end into a double eye by wrapping it around a piece of pipe. If you try this, drill a hole in the pipe to

catch the end of the wire, make the double turn, and then snip off the bit of wire in the hole (see drawing, facing page). We tie a label to the eye with insulated wire salvaged from phone cable. These markers last—we have 3,000 of them. True, in winter the plantings look like "a cemetery for mice," but we can identify the plants.

Labels are vital, but so are records. We keep a card on every plant in the garden, and we also keep plant maps, which are crucial when a thoughtless visitor pulls up a marker.

Ann Cummings

Considering my budget and the great many labels and markers I use, I've had to find a way to make my own out of easily available, and preferably free, materials. I use labels and markers to identify the hundreds of seedlings I start every spring, as well as perennial plants like shrubs, and large annuals like the eight or nine tomato varieties I grow each year, which can make even tall white stakes disappear.

For shrubs and trees, I make long-lasting aluminum labels. I set an aluminum pie plate on some newspapers, and write the plant names on it in indented letters by pressing hard with an old ball-point pen. Then I cut the plate into strips or plaques. I punch a hole in each label with an ice pick and tie the label to the plant with a strip of panty hose (which lasts for years and stretches). For extra legibility, you can write over the name with a marking pen, but this eventually fades. The indented letters last forever. The great virtue of these labels is that you

can make them any size or shape, as discreet or as visible as you like.

I make seedling markers by the hundreds every spring from white-plastic yogurt, cheese or margarine containers cut into strips with scissors, and write on them with a freezer pen. I use the markers in cell-packs and in the garden. When I clean up the garden in fall, I gather the markers and wash them for reuse, or slip them into my seed-collection envelopes for the following spring.

For large vegetables, I've switched to labels. My little seedling markers tended to disappear in the greenery, and there's almost nothing more frustrating than not knowing exactly which variety of pepper or broccoli is doing so much better than the others. I tried stakes of various kinds, but they'd get knocked over or lost in the mulch. Then I happened on bright-red plastic surveyor's tape. I cut 8-in.-long pieces and write on them with a freezer pen. With tomatoes I first tie a label around the base of each seedling and later move the flags to the tops of the tomato cages. Now I can tell whether the first ripe fruits come from 'Early Girl' or 'Santiam', and if that huge one was a 'Delicious' or a 'Supersteak'.

With smaller plants like peppers or broccoli, I just leave the tape tied loosely at the base of the stem. It may get covered by mulch, but it remains attached and I know exactly where to find it. At the end of the season when I pull up entire small hot-pepper plants to dry, they're already labeled. In the past, I always forgot to label dahlias by color before frost. Now I tie a tape label around each plant. When I dig the tubers to store them for the winter, the label comes along. I also use tape to mark squash or ears of corn that I've hand-pollinated and am saving for seeds.

There are tradeoffs among looks, legibility and visibility. I want visibility in the vegetable garden, no question about it. But for perennials, shrubs and trees, I prefer inconspicuous labels. Sometimes they're so inconspicuous that I can't find them. But I keep a plan of the permanent plantings, and record everything—well, almost everything—on it.

Alva G. Rosebrough

The search for the perfect marker is dear to my heart. During 50 years of gardening, I've tried many commercial and homemade versions, both outdoors and in the greenhouse. Today I make my own markers and labels from salvaged scraps of vinyl or aluminum house siding. I don't think you can improve on these materials for last-ability, legibility and economy.

Fabrication is easy. I make markers 6 in. to 12 in. long from aluminum siding, cutting the pieces with large household scissors and trimming the sharp corners for safety. Then I crimp the pieces on the diagonal so they're stiff enough to push into the soil. I make labels 4 in. to 6 in. long from either vinyl or aluminum siding. I tape about 20 together at a time and drill a 1/8-in. hole near one end. For label "wire," I use 3/32-in. heliarc aluminum filler rod, available at welding-supply houses. It lasts forever. The rod is soft and easy to loop over a twig or a stem. I also make markers with aluminum nameplates and U-shaped stanchions of aluminum rod (see photo at right).

I write on my markers and labels with marking pens. The letters stay legible for three to six years in my garden.

Patricia Steinbom

Of all the markers I've tried, I'm happiest with the ones I use now. Garden visitors frequently ask where I bought them, never suspecting that they were homemade by my father. I'm proud of his markers. They're simple, attractive and far less expensive than comparable manufactured markers. If you're even a little handy, you can make your own.

Before my father stepped in, the markers I used proved short-lived. Wooden stakes soon rotted. Even the best plastic markers became very brittle and broke easily after a season's exposure to the sun. Some inexpensive metal markers that were advertised as "permanent" proved to be temporary. The nameplates fell off, and the wire stems were very weak. I tried making markers out of discarded venetian blinds and plastic food trays from the supermarket, but the blinds quickly rusted and the plastic deteriorated. Besides, they looked tacky.

When I finally found long-lasting markers, the cost brought me up short. I purchased several dozen "deluxe" plant markers. They were just what I wanted. But as I became involved in collecting and hybridizing daylilies, I needed more markers than I could afford. Happily, my father looked at them and said, "I can make all you need." And he did.

My father's markers each consist of a stem made from stout rust-resistant wire and an aluminum nameplate. To make them, he uses wire cutters, metal snips, pliers, hammer, vise and drill. The stems are 9-ga. galvanized wire, which can be found at farm-supply stores. A 10-lb. roll costs less than $7 and will make enough stems for approximately 125 markers. Cut the wire into 21-in. lengths. At the top of each, make a 1/2-in. right-angle bend. This helps hold the nameplate in place. Make a 1-in. half-circle bend 4 in. from the bottom, which will help stabilize the stem in the ground. My father uses the vise in straightening the wire and making the bends.

For nameplates, you can buy aluminum at a sheet-metal shop, or for very little cost at a salvage yard, but the best source is a siding dealer, who is likely to have scrap pieces free for the asking. The white or colored finish of the siding makes an attractive surface that's easy to write on. To write on the nameplates, I use china markers. They're inexpensive and available locally at office-supply stores, and they make long-lasting, legible letters.

Cut out the nameplates to suit your taste, but add 1/4 in. top and bottom for folds. Drill a hole at the bottom for the wire stem to pass through. Bend the bottom 1/4 in. back at a right angle. Insert the stem and bend the top down securely over the wire to hold it in place. Again, the bends are made with the aid of a vise. Bend the wire stem so the nameplate is held at an angle for easy viewing. You're done, and the marker should last a lifetime. □

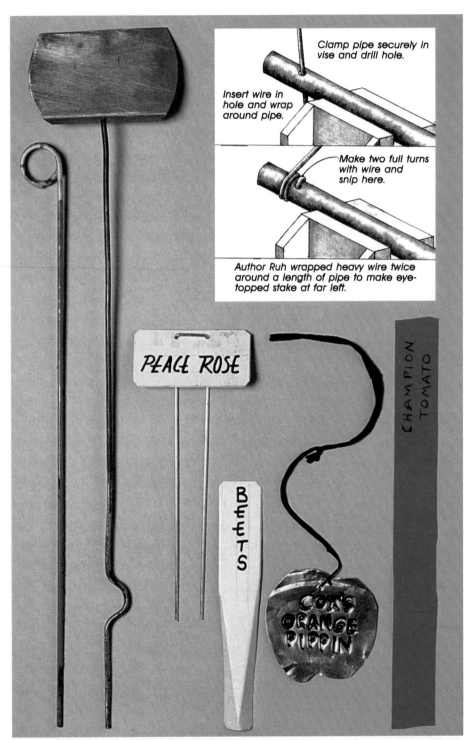

Clamp pipe securely in vise and drill hole.

Insert wire in hole and wrap around pipe.

Make two full turns with wire and snip here.

Author Ruh wrapped heavy wire twice around a length of pipe to make eye-topped stake at far left.

PEACE ROSE

BEETS

CHAMPION TOMATO

COX'S ORANGE PIPPIN

Homemade labels and markers: Four readers make these labels and markers, shown two-fifths life size. Peter Ruh ties a label to the eye of his stake (at left); the drawing shows how to make it. Patricia Steinborn's tall marker is 9-ga. galvanized wire and salvaged sheet aluminum. Alva Rosebrough's white marker and label are aluminum siding and 3/32-in. aluminum rod. Ann Cummings makes labels of red surveyor's tape, or aluminum pie plate with strips of panty hose for ties.

Drawing the Line
Choosing and installing
strip edgings

by Donald F. Ritterbusch

As a boy growing up on the East Coast, I lived in a beautiful home with a yard blessed with rich, black soil and filled with a wide variety of lush plants. Roses, irises, strawberries, blueberries, azaleas, rhododendrons and other wonderful plants each occupied their own separate garden. Each garden had a beautifully defined edge between the bright-green lawn and the dark, freshly tilled earth. The edge wasn't created by steel or wood or brick, but by the diligent and calloused hands of the full-time gardener, who employed a straight-edged shovel and a lot of effort to keep the gardens so well manicured.

As the family's only son, I was that gardener. The hours I spent at the end of that spade were not nearly as long and tedious as they seemed back then. They did, however, provide me with my first lessons in horticulture, and taught me to appreciate the fruit of hard work, as well as the value of a functional and permanent landscape edging.

Edging materials for separating lawns from planting beds have come far since those days nearly 30 years ago. In my career as a landscape designer and contractor in Colorado and throughout the Rocky Mountain West, I've installed miles of different edgings, and observed how they perform in home and commercial landscapes. I generally prefer the low, narrow profile of manufactured strip edgings made of steel, aluminum or polyethylene. They are simple to install along both curves and straight lines, they're easy to mow over and around, and they serve for years with minimum maintenance.

Scalloped cinder blocks, untreated 2x4s or other lightweight boards, thin corrugated aluminum, or reprocessed low-grade polyethylene should never be considered for use as a landscape edging by serious gardeners. The only advantage of these products is their low initial cost. They're hard to mow around and maintain. Small, narrow or lightweight edgings don't confine grass roots, and they shift and heave as the ground freezes and thaws with the seasons.

A good edging prevents lawn grass and other garden plants from spreading into each other's territories. Of course, some particularly invasive plants can breach an edging, but at least it will serve to slow them down. I think it's easier to trim back plants that have spread over the top of an edging than it is to pull out roots that

Polyethylene edging is an inexpensive and long-lasting material for separating turf grass from planting beds (above).

have burrowed underneath, so I recommend edgings with a minimum depth of 4½ in. Those 5 in. or 6 in. deep are even better, though installing them requires much more labor.

The top of the edging should lie just above the sod root zone, but down out of the way of the lawn mower. (Polyethylene can protrude higher than steel or aluminum.) On the planting-bed side, the soil level should be an inch or two lower than it is on the sod side. This helps to retain the bed aggregate and also discourages the spread of grass. Any stolons that cross the edging will be suspended in air, which will slow their tendency to root into the planting-bed soil.

Edgings usually are installed in trenches. All edgings must be staked to hold them in place, whether the manufacturer says so or not. This is especially true in heavy, expansive soils, or where the ground freezes and thaws repeatedly in the winter, causing the edging to lift above the sod level. It's good to tamp the soil firmly into place around an edging when you backfill a trench, but without stakes, tamping isn't adequate to hold an edging securely.

Installing edging takes time and care. Plan to work with one or two helpers, and set aside a whole day for the job. The most convenient time to install an edging is when you're preparing beds and starting a lawn. You don't have to watch where you step, and it's easier to dig trenches in loose, freshly prepared soil. If you're working around established plantings and sod, you have to be more attentive as you dig, and you're bound to disturb the soil, roots, and irrigation lines or sprinkler systems. Repairing or replacing a section of edging that's bent or broken or has shifted is hardest of all, because it's tough to get the new piece right in line and level with the old. Although it is possible to pull up, straighten out, rebend and reinstall any of these edgings if you change your mind about the outlines of your beds, it's a lot of trouble.

If your project requires many long, straight runs on level ground, steel is the simplest and fastest edging to install. High-grade polyethylene and aluminum edgings can also form a straight edge, but they're fussier to install than steel. It's also easy to bend steel around tight turns and sharp corners. Heavy-gauge aluminum edging is more rigid than steel, so it's less willing to bend into tight curves or corners. High-grade poly products are flexible enough to follow tight curves, but to form angles, corners and intersections, you need an appropriate connector joint.

It's challenging to edge a bed on a hilly site, where the edging has to climb a rounded slope. Polyethylene edging has some "give" and will flex slightly to accommodate grade changes. The only way you can run steel and aluminum

edgings over a curved surface is by splicing together a series of short pieces. Cutting metal edging is slow and vexing work, and the overlapped joints are liable to look awkward and require frequent maintenance to keep them in line.

Steel edging is most popular with professional landscape contractors here in the West. It combines simple installation, neat and unobtrusive appearance, long life expectancy, and ease of maintenance. I remember when steel edging was introduced in Denver more than 15 years ago. The Engbar Pipe and Steel Company had a surplus of 14-gauge, rolled black steel and marketed it to landscape contractors. Each piece had to be individually cut with a hacksaw from a huge coiled bundle weighing nearly a ton, with the ever-present danger of the bundle springing open like a coiled snake and injuring anyone within striking distance. Cutting was extremely tedious and time-consuming. The severed strips retained a memory of their curved storage, and therefore were quite difficult to handle, transport and install.

Today, steel edging comes in two forms, strip and prefabricated. Both are usually available in 10-ft. to 20-ft. lengths, 4 in. to 6 in. wide. Sections of strip steel are plain flat rectangles that you join by overlapping and anchor with U stakes that look like 18-in.-long bobby pins (see photo and drawings, pp. 70-71). Sections of prefab steel join together with precut scarf joints, anchored by 16-in.-long flat stakes that fit securely in punched-out holding strips. Both types of steel edging are available in 14-gauge thickness (about 1/16 in.), which I prefer for home gardens. Thinner 16- or 18-gauge metal does not hold up well, especially in more acid soils, and it's more liable to bend and buckle during installation. Steel manufacturers recommend the thicker gauges—up to ¼ in. thick, especially for commercial applications—but that thick steel is much heavier and harder to cut and handle.

The availability of steel edging varies around the country; check with garden centers, home-building suppliers or landscape contractors in your area. The edging itself generally costs between 35¢ and 45¢ per foot. Stakes for steel edging cost about 20¢ to 25¢ apiece.

Steel is called "black" in its unpainted, ungalvanized and untreated form; of course, black steel changes color as it rusts. Black steel will last for decades in dry, alkaline soils, but may rust out after several years in a moist, highly acid soil. The gauge of the metal, amount of rainfall or irrigation, drainage rate, soil pH and chemical applications all affect the longevity of steel in the ground. Painted and galvanized steels are often described as more durable, but the surface treat-

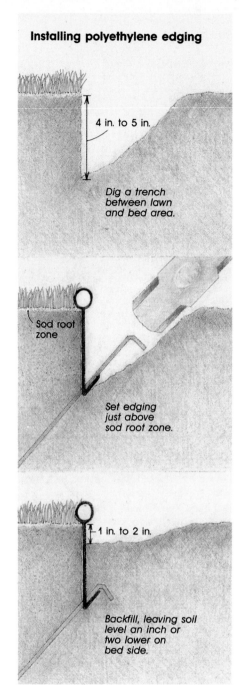

Installing polyethylene edging

4 in. to 5 in.

Dig a trench between lawn and bed area.

Sod root zone

Set edging just above sod root zone.

1 in. to 2 in.

Backfill, leaving soil level an inch or two lower on bed side.

ments that produce them are no guarantee against eventual corrosion. Rust isn't a serious problem here in Colorado, and I prefer the subtle, inconspicuous appearance of plain black steel. Green paint, intended to protect the raw steel and to allow the edging to blend into the lawn, often looks unnaturally bright. And it soon begins to chip and flake, becoming even more unsightly. The galvanized steel is no better. Its bright silver-colored coating can chip and flake off, particularly if the edging is pounded into the ground with a steel hammer during installation or after frost heave.

Strips of steel edging are heavy and ungainly, and the thin edges make steel dangerous to carry. Wear leather gloves, solid boots or shoes, and a long-sleeved

Here are four professional-grade edging products and their stakes (left to right): Black Diamond polyethylene, Permaloc aluminum, strip steel (with plastic safety strip), and Ryerson prefabricated steel.

shirt while you're handling it. In soft or friable soils, you can simply pound strip steel edging into place, cushioning the blows of the sledge hammer with a wooden block. In hard soils, heavy clay or rocky areas, you'll have to dig a trench to install it. Steel is flexible enough to follow curved outlines. To make sharp angles, just hammer it around the corner of a wooden block. I use a hacksaw or a cutting torch to cut steel edging to length. Either method leaves a ragged burr, but nobody I know takes the time to file this off. It's a good idea, however, to miter or round off the top corner when you make a cut, rather than leaving a sharp point.

When placing strip steel, be sure to overlap the strips at least 6 in. and to use two stakes on the joint (drawing, facing page). The stakes will grip the edging and stay in place better if you pound the bent end into a tighter crook before you hammer them down into the ground. A stake every 5 ft. is usually sufficient for straight runs, but put them closer together on curves.

You'll need to dig a trench to install prefabricated steel edging. The prepunched stake holes will be your guide for joining the sections, since they must line up for proper fit. Position the stakes through the holes and drive them in place before backfilling the trench. The prefab steel stakes do a better job of securing the edging and withstanding frost heave than U stakes do. But if in cutting to length you cut off the prepunched stake holes, use U stakes to secure the end of the edging.

Even though steel is arguably a superior edging product, it does have its hazards. The long edges aren't sharp like a knife, but tripping or landing on the metal could cause serious injury. I highly recommend buying an inexpensive plastic safety strip (which costs less than 20¢ per foot) that fits over the top edge of new or

existing steel. Steel edgings are also very susceptible to frost heave and sinkage. When the edging heaves and projects above grade level, it can trip pedestrians, unsuspecting children and pets. Along driveways, uplifted steel can cut into tires. Check the edging periodically, and tap it back into place with a hammer where needed. Before mowing, always walk around and check steel edging. Be *sure* it is down out of the way. Striking steel edging with a lawn mower can injure the mower, the mower operator or bystanders.

Aluminum edging comes in two distinctly different versions. The lightweight, corrugated aluminum edging sold at discount stores is as short-lived as it is inexpensive. Professional-grade aluminum edging is something else again—it's a heavy-duty, high-tech product. The only heavy-gauge aluminum edging available at this time is manufactured by Permaloc (13505 Barry St., Holland, MI 49424; phone collect, 616-399-9600, for the location of the distributor nearest you).

Permaloc aluminum edging is still new on the market, so I haven't had much experience with it yet. It looks like a very interesting alternative to steel edging. Lengthwise grooves and ridges in the strips, and barbs on the fastening stakes are designed to hold the edging in place and resist frost heaving. The joints where the strips fasten together are slightly loose, so the edging can shift a bit when frost changes the soil, and then settle back in place again when the ground thaws out. Aluminum doesn't rust, and it has a very high resistance to corrosion from salts from deicers and fertilizers. Permaloc edging is rounded on top, so it's not liable to cut feet.

Unfortunately, Permaloc costs five to 15 times as much as steel edging. The extra expense might make sense in regions

with moist, acid soil, which will quickly deteriorate steel. So far, Permaloc has been used mostly by professional landscapers, but it's becoming increasingly available to homeowners from garden centers and landscape contractors. It comes in either a natural silver color or an anodized black, and in ⅛-in. and ³⁄₁₆-in. thicknesses, 4-in. and 5½-in. widths, and manageable 16-ft. lengths. Retail price for these different versions runs between $2.80 and $6.00 a foot. (The black finish costs about 15% more than the silvery finish.) Plain stakes cost less than $2 apiece, and splicer stakes (to connect two sections together) cost about $2.50 each.

You need to dig a trench for the original installation, but you can use a hammer to tamp the edging back in place if it does heave. The manufacturer claims that Permaloc is faster and easier to install than prefabricated steel edging. I didn't find this to be true for the few sections I installed; however, I could see that proficiency would come with practice. Permaloc isn't nearly as forgiving as steel or polyethylene. Once two strips are connected, they are very difficult to separate. Of course, this would be an advantage when they're properly installed.

Polyethylene edging has been much maligned through the years, due to the commonly accepted but untrue notion that all plastic is junk. There are reprocessed plastic edgings, which quickly discolor, harden and crack when exposed to the sun; some even deteriorate within months of installation. And they are liable to kink or break if you bend them around tight curves. Virgin polyethylene edging, however, is a high-density plastic, usually containing additives to resist ultraviolet deterioration. It is pliable, stable and durable—in some installations, it has lasted more than ten or 15 years.

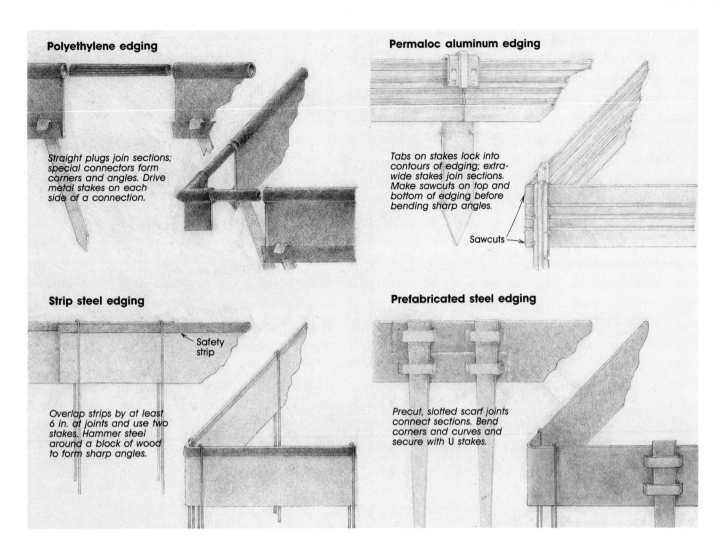

Polyethylene edging

Straight plugs join sections; special connectors form corners and angles. Drive metal stakes on each side of a connection.

Permaloc aluminum edging

Tabs on stakes lock into contours of edging; extra-wide stakes join sections. Make sawcuts on top and bottom of edging before bending sharp angles.

Sawcuts

Strip steel edging

Safety strip

Overlap strips by at least 6 in. at joints and use two stakes. Hammer steel around a block of wood to form sharp angles.

Prefabricated steel edging

Precut, slotted scarf joints connect sections. Bend corners and curves and secure with U stakes.

The quality of the plastic, therefore, is the most important factor to consider when choosing and buying polyethylene edging. I recommend edgings from two manufacturers, Valley View Specialties (13834 S. Kostner, Crestwood, IL 60445; phone 800-323-9369) and Oly-Ola Sales (54 East St. Charles Rd., Villa Park, IL 60181; phone 800-334-4647). Available at many garden centers, theirs and other name-brand plastic edgings are far superior to cheap "generic" edgings, but cost only slightly more. Top-quality edging strips cost between 40¢ and 70¢ per foot. Stakes run about 50¢ apiece, and angle or corner connectors are about $2.50 each.

Plastic edgings are lightweight and easy to handle, and they don't rust or corrode. They are arguably the safest edgings—they have no sharp edges, corners or splinters, and all stakes are buried below the ground. If you inadvertently strike the top of the edging with a mower blade, you'll only lose a chunk of plastic. Of course, after this has happened a few times, the edging will start to look shabby and won't function as well. Likewise, if installed along a sidewalk or a driveway, plastic edgings can get torn up in the winter months by snow shovels and blow-

ers. Plastic isn't the strongest edging material, so don't install it where heavy equipment such as cars, trucks or riding lawn mowers will repeatedly run over it.

Plastic edgings aren't just flat strips; most types have grooves and ridges down the length of the sections, or large, angular fins protruding along the base. These add structural integrity and help weather frost heaving. Most also have rounded tops that are tubular or S-shaped. These configurations give strength and stability to the edgings, but many gardeners disdain the appearance of the exposed round top, saying it looks like a length of black plastic pipe running along the bed. Actually, there is a model of edging where the tubular top doubles as a water line for a drip irrigation system. This might sound like a good idea, but in most areas of the country an above-ground water line is liable to freeze and break if it's not drained.

Most plastic edging comes in strips 10 ft., 20 ft. or 25 ft. long. It's easy to coil up the strips to fit in the back of a station wagon, but you should straighten them out again as soon as possible, before they develop a "memory" for the coiled position. Some brands are rolled and boxed, which

makes them easier to buy and carry home, but harder to uncoil and use. Putting them out in the hot sun will soften the plastic a little if you're having trouble straightening the strips.

To cut the edging into shorter lengths, use a hacksaw or a sharp knife. Use the manufacturer's connectors to join sections, or to form acute- or right-angle turns or tees. For short, close or curved areas, I install just one section at a time. You can connect several sections together before you lower them into the trench for long, straight runs.

Plastic edging must be installed in a trench, and it must be secured with long, wide and slightly dished stakes. Position the edging with the bottom fin facing toward the softer soil inside the planting bed. Drive the stakes through the edging, and angle them down and out into the firmer soil under the sod. Use stakes every 5 ft. along a straight run, closer together around curves. If you secure polyethylene edging with plenty of stakes when you install it, it will stay in place for years. □

Don Ritterbusch is editor of Colorado Green, *the magazine of the Associated Landscape Contractors of Colorado.*

Pressure-treated Lumber

Long life and versatility for garden construction

by Mark Kane

Pressure-treated lumber has transformed the way gardeners use wood. Though 50% more expensive than ordinary lumber, pressure-treated lumber is far longer-lived outdoors, especially in damp conditions and in contact with the ground. Preservatives driven into the wood protect it from insects and decay for decades. Sold in sizes ranging from 2 × 2s for balusters to 6 × 6s for stockade fences, pressure-treated lumber lends itself to all sorts of garden projects, including straight or curved retaining walls, garden furniture, decks and patios, planters, fences, edging, latticework, arbors, compost bins and trellises.

Pressure treatment

Given oxygen, warm temperatures and moisture, decay-producing fungi and insects soon destroy wood's strength and appearance. Wood in contact with the ground is at high risk, especially in the top 6 in. of soil, where oxygen and moisture are abundant. Above ground, wood decays more slowly, provided conditions are usually dry.

The most effective way of protecting lumber from decay and insect damage is pressure treatment with a wood preservative. Sealed inside a steel cylinder, lumber is subjected to a vacuum, which pulls air from the wood. Then the cylinder is filled with wood preservative and pressurized to drive the preservative into the lumber.

By far the most common and suitable wood preservative for residential lumber is chromated copper arsenate (CCA), a mix of salts or oxides of copper, chromium and arsenic. More than 95% of the pressure-treated lumber sold for residential use is treated with CCA, which binds chemically to wood, does not vaporize or leach, and does not harm nearby plants. The three elements in CCA have different ef-

A wooden planter provides a level bed for asparagus in a sloping yard. Because pressure-treated lumber resists decay, the planter will remain attractive for decades. It has been painted with a water-repellent stain, which will not crack or blister.

fects. Copper inhibits growth of decay fungi (and gives CCA-treated lumber a characteristic greenish tinge); arsenic kills wood-eating insects; and chromium is thought to bind CCA to wood.

Lumberyards sell two types of CCA-treated lumber, one for aboveground uses and the other for ground contact. The two types differ in the amount of CCA they retain after pressure treatment, measured in pounds of CCA per cubic foot of wood. For aboveground uses, treated lumber must retain .25 lb. of CCA per cubic foot. For ground contact, the retention must be .40 lb./cu. ft.

Pressure-treated lumber is widely available in a range of sizes. You can find 2 × 2s to 2 × 12s and fence posts and timbers from 4 × 4s to 6 × 6s. There are also so-called landscape timbers, which

are the leftover cores of logs sliced for veneer, with two flat faces and two curved faces. For fence boards and decking, there are .25 retention planks. And there are a number of specialty items, such as .25 retention balusters and handgrips for porch railings, .25 retention lattices of crisscrossing wood strips in sheets 2 ft. or 4 ft. wide by 8 ft. long, and .40 retention plywood for ground contact.

When you shop for treated lumber, make sure each piece carries a quality stamp or tag, and read it closely. Look first for assurance that the pressure treatment meets industry standards. You should see the initials or trademark of an industry inspection agency, or the name of a proprietary CCA treatment, such as Osmose, Koppers, or Wolmanized. Among overseers' groups, the American Wood

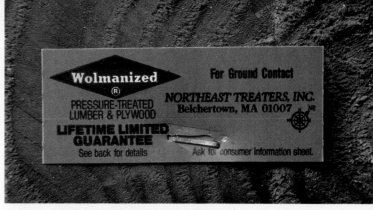

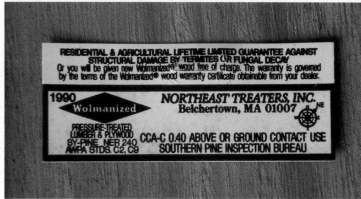

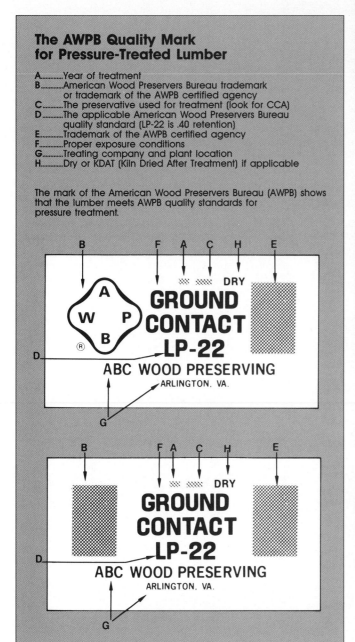
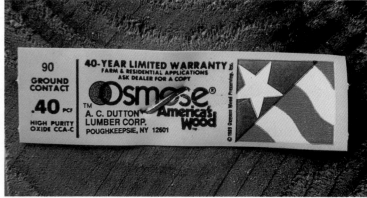

The front (top) and back (middle) of this tag show that the lumber has been treated for ground contact with CCA (chromated copper arsenate, the most common wood preservative). "Wolmanized" is a proprietary name of the CCA manufacturer, and 0.40 is the pounds of preservative per cubic foot of lumber. The yellow tag (bottom) also indicates treatment for ground contact; "Osmose" is a proprietary name.

Preservers Bureau (AWPB) is widely acknowledged as the most independent. It operates a testing laboratory and certifies inspection agencies that stamp or tag properly-treated lumber with their trademark. For a list of AWPB-certified agencies, write to AWPB, P.O. Box 5283, Springfield, VA 22150. The Southern Pine Inspection Bureau also certifies inspection agencies. For a list, write SPIB, 4709 Scenic Highway, Pensacola, FL 32504-9094.

The stamp or tag on pressure-treated lumber should also show a retention number, either .25 or .40, and the initials CCA. Since CCA is manufactured in several forms, the tag may say "CCA oxides," "CCA-C," or another variation. All the forms of CCA provide similar protection. Instead of a retention number, some stamps or tags show an AWPB code. LP-2

indicates .25 retention, and LP-22 indicates .40 retention.

Beware of stamps and tags that say "treated to refusal" or that identify only the treatment plant. Self-labelled lumber may be properly treated, but it has not been inspected by a second party. Lumber "treated to refusal" carries no assurance that the wood retains enough preservative for long life in outdoor uses.

Longevity

The longevity of pressure-treated lumber depends on the type of wood, the treatment, and how the lumber will be used. We know a lot about longevity thanks to research by the Forest Products Laboratory, a branch of the USDA, with headquarters in Madison, Wisconsin. Applying what we know to a 2 × 6 in the

lumberyard, however, amounts to educated guesswork.

The Forest Products Laboratory maintains a long-running experiment with pressure-treated 2 × 4 stakes in Mississippi. Dried and then treated to .40 retention, the 2 × 4s were set in the ground 43 years ago. At intervals, the stakes are pulled up and inspected for decay and insect damage. In spite of Mississippi's warm, humid climate and active termites, to date not one of the 43-year-old pressure-treated 2 × 4s has failed. On the same site, untreated 2 × 4s fail within one to three years. The pressure-treated stakes are still intact for two reasons: they were thoroughly dry before treatment, and they contain no heartwood.

How does drying lumber before pressure treatment affect longevity? The in-

Here are two pressure-treated 2 x 4s, cut from different parts of the tree. The one on the right bisects the center of the tree and is mainly heartwood, while the one on the left, from the outer layers of the tree, is mostly sapwood. Pressure treatment penetrates sapwood far more deeply than heartwood, so the 2 x 4 on the left is likely to resist decay more completely than the 2 x 4 on the right.

dustry does not dry lumber before treatment as thoroughly as the FPL dried its 2 × 4 stakes 43 years ago. The industry aims for lumber at 15% moisture before treatment; the FPL dried its 2 × 4s to 6.8% moisture. In service, most pressure-treated lumber develops cracks as it dries and shrinks. Since preservative penetrates only partway into most pressure-treated lumber, a deep crack can expose untreated wood and shorten the service life of the lumber.

How does heartwood affect longevity? Sapwood is the younger, outer layers of a tree. Heartwood is the older and often darker core, which is usually laden with natural wood preservatives. Pressure treatment penetrates sapwood more readily than heartwood. The difference is significant. While industry standards call for CCA-treated lumber to show 2½ in. of sapwood penetration (or 85% of sapwood thinner than 2½ in.), the penetration in heartwood can be as little as ½ in. Heartwood has its own preservatives, but they are less effective than CCA. If a crack extends into untreated heartwood, decay soon starts, and the heartwood can rot in seven years or less. In practical terms, a treated 2 × 4 that is all sapwood is likely to outlast one that is part sapwood and part heartwood.

When you're turning over boards at the lumberyard, look first for the lumber with the most sapwood. Check the growth rings on the end of each piece. If you see full circles, you are looking at the center of the tree. If you see sharp arcs that would make circles 2 in. to 6 in. in diameter, you are probably looking at heartwood. Growth rings with broader arcs indicate sapwood. You're most likely to find all-sapwood lumber in the smallest sizes—2 × 4s, 2 × 6s, 1 × planks, railings and balusters. Larger sizes almost always

Creosote and pentachlorophenol

Two widely-used wood preservatives are ill-suited for treating lumber that will be used in the garden. One is creosote, or coal tar, a pungent-smelling liquid, distilled from coal, that was the first preservative used in pressure treatment (in 1865, for railroad ties). Another is pentachlorophenol, penta for short, from a family of compounds that includes the herbicides 2,4-D and 2,4,5-T. Both preservatives are used mainly on lumber for industry—power poles, railroad ties, heavy timbers and the like, which you are not likely to find at a homeowners' lumberyard.

If you happen to buy lumber recently treated with creosote or pentachlorophenol, heed a few cautions. Creosote and pentachlorophenol can be absorbed through the skin; the EPA advises wearing rubber gloves and protective clothing to handle treated lumber. Freshly-treated lumber can harm or kill nearby plants, since both preservatives leach from treated lumber and both produce herbicidal vapor. Salvaged railroad ties, though treated with creosote, are an exception—once they have weathered for years, they produce very little vapor. Lumber treated with penta and creosote must not be used where it can contact bare skin or where animals may bite or lick the wood, unless it is painted with an effective sealer, such as shellac or epoxy paint.   —M.K.

have some heartwood, and timbers often contain the center of the tree. Try to select pieces that are largely sapwood, with the heartwood on or near the edge, so decay in the heartwood will not destroy their strength. If appearance counts, face the heartwood away from view.

For long service, cut treated lumber as little as possible since notching and cutting can expose untreated wood. Size your project to use standard lumber lengths. Instead of notching a post to support a rail, bolt the rail to the post.

If you cut or bore a piece of pressure-treated wood, paint the exposed surfaces with zinc or copper napthenate (preservatives sold by well-stocked lumberyards) or any of the many brand-name water repellents which are basically a mix of wax, rosin and solvent that soaks into wood and seals the surface. (For more information, send for "Wood Finishing: Water Repellents and Water-Repellent Preservatives," from Forest Products Laboratory, Forest Service, U.S. Department of Agriculture, Madison, WI 53705.) Brush on the preservative or repellent generously, let it soak in, and repeat.

Lee R. Gjovic, who retired as head of FPL's preservative group, has a surprising tip if you have to cut a fencepost—"Put the cut end in the ground," he says. As long as the posthole is at least 18 in. deep, there's little risk of decay, even if the cut exposes untreated wood, because there is too little oxygen in most soils below 18 in. to support decay organisms.

Recently, some wood treaters have begun offering warranties for pressure-treated lumber. Are they guaranteeing longevity? No. Gjovic says, "A warranty is a marketing ploy, pure and simple. All it says is they'll replace a piece of lumber if it fails before 40 years are up, provided you are the original buyer and you have the sales slip and the quality tag." Gjovic also warns that warranties are limited. If a post fails and your porch sags, the warranty merely replaces the post.

Safety
The EPA has ruled that CCA-treated lumber, when properly handled and used, is safe for people and the environment. Under a voluntary agreement with the EPA, the treatment industry supplies lumberyards with a sheet of guidelines for proper handling and use of treated lumber. Ask your lumberyard for the Consumer Information Sheet (CIS).

What precautions should you take in handling and using pressure-treated lumber? First, buy lumber that looks clean. Avoid pieces with a dusty surface, because lumber sometimes emerges from pressure-treatment with a surface residue of CCA. It should be cleaned before shipment, but occasionally a piece slips through. Second, wear gloves when handling pressure-treated lumber. Though the EPA says that little or no arsenic is absorbed from contact with treated wood, minimizing exposure is simple prudence. Third, avoid inhaling sawdust. Wear a mask when cutting treated wood and sweeping up sawdust, and do the cutting outdoors to keep sawdust out of your house. Bag sawdust and scraps and send them to the dump. Do not burn them—burning releases toxic compounds into the air. When working with treated lumber, wash your hands before eating, drinking or smoking, and wash work clothes separately from other laundry.

Research indicates that CCA-treated lumber can be used safely near plants. The FPL test in Mississippi has shown that soil alongside pressure-treated stakes picks up negligible quantities of CCA. Right next to the stakes, there are barely-measurable amounts of CCA; one inch from the stakes, there is no trace of CCA. In a separate university-conducted test, grapevines trained on CCA-treated posts showed no trace of the preservative, and no change in growth.

If you are wary of pressure-treated lumber, however, you do have other options. For many aboveground uses, you can paint ordinary lumber with a clear or pigmented water repellent. For dependable protection, you must repaint every two to three years. Water repellents, however, have limits: they will not protect wood that is constantly wet or surrounded by humid air—for example, the bottom of a trellis a few inches from the soil. For ground contact, you can substitute other building materials. For example, you might cast a planter in concrete, pour concrete pilings to support a low deck, or lay stones for a retaining wall.

Though a few woods—among them, cypress, cedar and redwood—have reputations for natural resistance to decay, their lumber is unlikely to provide long service. Only the heartwood possesses enough resistance for outdoor use, and few lumberyards sell heartwood lumber. You can order redwood lumber that consists entirely of heartwood, and it may approach pressure-treated lumber for longevity, but it is a dwindling resource and far more expensive than pressure-treated lumber. Most cypress, cedar and redwood lumber is a mix of heartwood and sapwood, unsuited to ground contact and unlikely to outlast pressure-treated lumber in garden use.

Fastening and painting

Fasteners for treated wood must be rust resistant. Exposed to weather, ordinary steel nails and bolts rust rapidly (incidentally disfiguring the wood with streaks). For aboveground lumber, use hot-dipped galvanized steel nails, screws and bolts. If the wood is constantly wet, use stainless-

Author Kane cuts a pressure-treated 2 x 4. Following EPA guidelines, he wears gloves to handle the wood and a mask to avoid inhaling sawdust.

steel fasteners. It's good practice to drill pilot holes for nails in pressure-treated wood, especially at the ends of boards, to avoid splitting the board and exposing untreated wood.

Though pressure-treated lumber resists decay, it weathers like untreated lumber. The surface breaks down and turns gray from exposure to the ultraviolet rays of sunlight. The wood absorbs rain and expands, then shrinks and cracks. Splits may develop in the ends of boards, and pieces may separate from the surface of some boards.

Painting pressure-treated lumber reduces weathering. You can use regular paint, the kind that forms a solid film, but Gjovic recommends a water repellent. It does not prevent surface cracks, but it does stop deep cracks, splits and separations. If you want color, buy a stain that combines pigment and a water repellent. The grain of the wood shows through a stain, but at a distance the color looks solid. Before you paint, test the stain on a scrap of wood—the green tint of treated lumber can alter the color. Brush on stain in continuous strokes to avoid overlaps. Good coverage may take several coats. Gjovic has some advice for areas that get foot traffic. "Color will show wear," he says. "Use a clear water repellent, one that contains a biocide to prevent mildew and mold, which grow on dust and dirt. When mold gets wet, it's slippery."

Paint pressure-treated lumber when the wood is dry. If it is wet, regular paint will adhere poorly or blister as moisture in the wood escapes, and water repellents will not soak into the wood evenly. Gjovic recommends you build your project, then let the lumber weather a year before you paint. Wait for the end of a hot, dry spell, if possible. □

Mark Kane is an associate editor at Fine Gardening *magazine.*

Controlling Weeds with Landscape Fabrics

How to use synthetic mulches

by Bonnie Lee Appleton

Most of us fight a constant battle to control weeds in our landscape because weeds look bad. Even more important than their poor appearance, though, is the damage weeds can do to ornamentals. Weeds compete with the plants we want to grow—for moisture, nutrients, space and light.

Weeds also can harbor insect and disease organisms that infest and infect ornamentals.

Popular controls include mulching to smother weeds, cultivating the soil, pulling out weeds by hand and applying preemergent or postemergent herbicides. Newer to the field of weed control are landscape fabrics, also called landscape fabric barriers or geotextiles. They can reduce the amount of manual weeding and chemical controls needed, but many gardeners don't take advantage of these barriers because they are confused about how to choose a landscape fabric and use it most effectively.

What are landscape fabrics?

Landscape fabrics are synthetic materials manufactured from petroleum products and are either woven, nonwoven or spunbonded. When they are laid on top of the soil, landscape fabrics form a physical barrier that keeps perennial weeds from sending foliage above the soil surface. They also exclude light, which prevents the seeds of annual

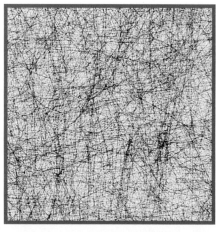
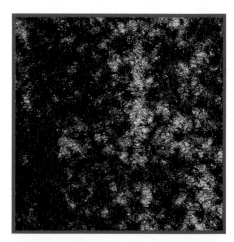
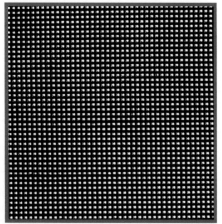
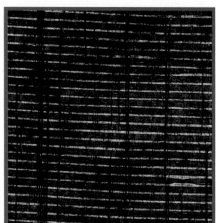
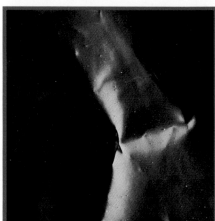

Landscape fabrics give long-term weed control and reduce the need for hand weeding and herbicides. Dense fabrics suppress more weeds, and dark ones do a better job of inhibiting weed seed germination. The fabrics in the top row are spunbonded polyethylene or polyester/polyethylene. In the bottom row, left-to-right, are embossed polyethylene film, woven polypropylene and black plastic.

Photos: Susan Kahn

weeds from germinating. At the same time, the fabrics are porous enough to allow water, air and nutrients to reach plant roots.

Since 1987, I've participated in an ongoing program to test and compare the effectiveness of landscape fabrics and traditional weed barrier mulches. Dr. Jeffrey Derr, Virginia Polytechnic Institute and State University's weed specialist for ornamental crops, is my partner in the project, which is sponsored by the Virginia Technical University, at the Hampton Roads Agricultural Experiment Station in Virginia Beach, Virginia.

Our aim is to set standards for the usage, effectiveness and durability of these products. Everything we learned could have been discovered in a home garden, but the scope of what we've done is greater. Our findings make it possible for me to read manufacturers' claims, compare them with our field observations and draw some conclusions.

We've tested over two dozen products, looking at how they controlled weeds and modified the soil environment and plant growth. While fabrics used alone can effectively suppress weeds, manufacturers recommend covering them with a loose mulch such as gravel, bark or pine needles to protect the synthetic fabrics from breakdown caused by ultraviolet light. Currently, we are comparing organic mulches to inorganic mulches set atop the fabrics, to determine which types of mulches best suppress weed growth while protecting the fabrics from deterioration by the elements. (See "Loose mulch toppings for fabric" on p. 79.)

The forerunner of today's landscape fabrics was opaque plastic film (polyethylene). This material is an effective weed barrier, but it has some drawbacks. It keeps water-soluble nutrients and air from reaching plant roots. It also prevents saturated soil from drying out and inhibits plant respiration by preventing the exchange of gases between the soil and the atmosphere. Our tests have not shown that short-term use of this material harms plants, but long-term use around perennial and woody landscape plants can lead to root problems, including carbon dioxide buildup in the soil, development of surface roots searching for adequate oxygen and overly-wet soil. High concentrations of carbon dioxide in the soil can be toxic to plants; surface roots can be damaged by drought, cold or cultivation; and water-logged soil can lead to root rot. Using porous fabric barriers can help you avoid some of these problems.

Installing a landscape fabric

Proper installation is the first step in successfully using landscape fabrics. I recommend placing them over weed-free ground. This requires that you first kill all existing vegetation by cultivation or with an herbicide. Fabric barriers can then be installed before or after planting.

If you install them *before* planting, cut holes or X-shaped slits, as small as possible, in the material. This minimizes the amount of exposed soil—a place for potential weed growth. Be sure about where you want to place the plants

before you make the cuts. Dig the planting holes before placing the fabric, marking each hole with a stake, or make an opening, no larger than necessary, in the fabric in order to dig each hole. But in either case, if you get soil on the fabric when digging, you should carefully remove it so that weeds can't grow in it. You don't want to rearrange the plants after cutting the holes—this will leave bare soil where weeds can grow. After planting, reposition the fabric to cover any exposed soil, or pin down the fabric at the base of each plant.

If installing a weed barrier *after* planting, which I generally recommend, you can estimate where to cut a hole or slit for each plant and then carefully fit the fabric down over the plants. This can be quite difficult if it's windy and you're working with a lightweight material, but I think it's worth the extra effort because this keeps the fabric free of soil and weed seed contamination. Narrow pieces of fabric must be overlapped or seamed to prevent weed growth between the pieces. Remember that woven fabrics may unravel if they're cut or handled excessively.

Loose mulch protects landscape fabrics from sun damage, as proved in test plots (above), and improves their appearance (below). Fabrics work best around permanent plantings. Overlap the edges so weeds won't grow through the seams.

Before you use one of these materials for a large planting, we recommend you try a small piece of one or more types in various areas of your landscape and note the results.

Mulching the fabric

After installing landscape fabrics, most people cover them with loose mulch to protect them against photodecomposition and to improve their appearance. Manufacturers usually recommend putting 1 in. to 3 in. of mulch atop the fabrics. Some fabrics are treated with stabilizers to retard UV breakdown; others aren't. Dark-colored fabrics, however, suppress weeds better than light or white fabrics because they block out more light. There are no industry standards regarding UV stabilizers in landscape fabrics. If the packaging doesn't clearly state that the product is treated, contact the manufacturer to find out.

I've discovered that covering landscape fabrics with mulch unfortunately can actually encourage the growth of weeds. Weed seeds may already be present in the organic mulch topping, or they may be carried

Photos: Bonnie Lee Appleton

The author's tests revealed tree and shrub root growth through some landscape fabrics (above). Pulling up the fabric damages roots. If weeds that grow in loose mulch topping aren't removed or killed when small, they can send roots through the fabrics. When pulled up, they often take sections of fabric with them, leaving large holes (below).

to the mulch by wind or irrigation, or in the soil surrounding the roots of a transplant.

Our tests show that weeds growing in the mulch layer often send roots down through landscape fabrics. Once the weeds root into the soil beneath the fabrics, they grow vigorously. If you pull these weeds, you're liable to rip the fabric, creating holes for future weed growth.

These fabrics are better at controlling annual than perennial weeds. Perennial weeds that spread by rhizomes or tubers are especially difficult for fabric barriers to contain. Some weeds will even grow under and eventually up through the fabrics. Nutsedge and bermudagrass (wiregrass), common perennial problem weeds in the Southeast, have grown up through every fabric we have tested.

Although many fabrics give less-than-perfect weed control, they don't create unfavorable soil conditions for plant roots. We compared plots covered with landscape fabrics that were topped with organic mulch to plots covered only with the same organic mulch, and found no significant difference between the two in soil moisture and temperature. All of our field-tested fabrics allowed adequate air and moisture exchange for good tree and shrub root growth.

After two years of testing, we did discover two potential problems, which we are now closely watching. First, we found tree and shrub roots growing through and on top of loosely constructed fabrics, and even into the mulch layer. It's not uncommon to find tree and shrub roots growing in organic mulch layers, just as they do in forest litter, because the moist,

SOURCES

The companies listed here sell fabric mulches retail, by mail-order, in participating garden centers or hardware stores. The manufacturers can provide information on construction, prices, shipping costs and guarantees.

Agri-Tex, Inc., P.O. Box 1106, Danbury, CT 06813. (800) 243-0989. Magic Mat brand. Catalog free.

Blunk's Wholesale Supply, Inc., 3145 W. Columbus Ave., Chicago IL 60652. Duon Landscape Fabric brand. Catalog free.

Dalen Products, Inc., 11110 Gilbert Dr., Knoxville, TN 37932-3099. (615) 966-3256. Weed-X brand. Catalog free.

DeWitt Co., Inc., Route 3, Box 338, Sikeston, MO 63801. (314) 472-0048. Weed Barrier brand. Catalog free.

Reemay, Inc., P.O. Box 511, 70 Old Hickory Blvd., Old Hickory, TN 37138. (615) 847-7000. Typar Landscape Fabric brand. Catalog free.

well-aerated conditions found there are conducive to root growth. However, we were concerned that some roots had actually grown backwards—up, into and through the open-weave fabrics. If you pull up the fabric, the interlaced roots could be damaged. At this time, we can only recommend using tightly woven or bonded fabrics around shrubs, trees or other permanent plantings, and leaving them in place to prevent damaging roots.

The other potential problem we encountered was an increase in vole runs under both black plastic and landscape fabrics that were covered with mulch. Voles, sometimes called field mice, are herbivores. These small rodents live throughout the country in grassy areas with regular rainfall, and they feed on tree roots and trunks at ground level. In our test plots, there were more vole runs under landscape fabrics than in bare soil, or where herbicides or loose mulches were used. In areas where these rodents exist, the fabrics may create favorable conditions for them.

Our recommendations

For best results, I suggest that you start out with a weed-free area. If your landscape fabric lacks UV stabilizers, cover it evenly with a 2-in. layer of mulch to prevent deterioration, and pull any weeds that crop up in the mulch topping while they are still small.

Although landscape fabrics are useful and cost-effective for long-term plantings, they are less effective when used around annuals (both flowers and vegetables), because it is necessary to cut many small holes. If you use fabrics with annuals, in following seasons the original holes that aren't filled with plants will become places where weeds can grow.

Landscape fabrics seem best suited for use around trees and shrubs, where only small increases in stem diameter occur each year. Landscape fabrics restrict clump expansion and stem rooting in ground covers, vines and perennials that spread by above- or below-ground roots.

Ultimately, whether you decide to use landscape fabrics in your weed control program will depend on plant spacing and permanence in your landscape, the amount of time you have for weeding and the availability and cost of these materials in your area. □

Bonnie Lee Appleton is an extension specialist with Virginia Polytechnic Institute and State University, Virginia Beach, Virginia, and an educational adviser to the Virginia Nurserymen's Association.

Loose mulch toppings for fabric

Manufacturers of fabric barriers suggest covering their products with mulches to protect the fabrics against photodecomposition (chemical breakdown initiated by exposure to the sun's ultraviolet rays) and to enhance their appearance.

Inorganic mulches such as gravel, marble chips or decorative stone made from volcanic materials are sometimes recommended because they don't contain material in which surface weeds can root. However, our tests showed that even when inorganic mulches are used, there is still some weed growth due to seeds, soil and organic matter blowing onto the inorganic mulches. Also, perennial weeds under the fabric can grow up through the barrier's fibers, despite mulching.

There are other disadvantages to inorganic mulches, too. Gardeners may find them unattractive. Limestone-based mulches (including gray and white marble chips) can alter soil pH when calcium leaches from them. At present, our research shows variation in the effectiveness of weed control among inorganic and organic mulches, depending on their particle size, depth of the mulch and the type of fabric beneath the mulch.

Inorganic mulches suppress weeds slightly better than organic mulches. In our tests, white marble chips inhibited weed growth best. Variously-colored volcanic (lava) rocks were second best.

Loose mulches protect landscape fabrics against sun damage. Clockwise, from left, according to their performance in the author's weed-control tests, are white marble chips, large chunks of pine bark, medium ground pine bark, and black and red volcanic rock.

Organic mulches such as bark, pine needles, leaf mold, straw or hay, peanut or rice hulls, mushroom compost, sawdust, tobacco stems and corncobs are considered by many gardeners to be more attractive than inorganic mulches because they have a more natural-looking color and texture. In our tests, however, results with organic mulches as weed inhibitors have been variable. Materials, such as shredded pine bark and composted leaf mold, tend to be cleaner, or have less weed-seed contamination, than straw and hardwood bark mulch. We recommend using the cleanest mulch available in your area for topping landscape fabrics.

Particle size seems to be important in organic mulches. Coarse mulches such as pine needles and chunk or nugget pine bark have given better weed control than shredded bark. The fine particles in shredded pine bark begin to decompose, producing a growing medium for weeds. When organic mulches are used without fabrics, decomposition may be desired so that organic matter can be incorporated into the soil, but this is not the case when fabrics are used.

With organic mulches, the depth to which you mulch depends on the particle size. Organic mulches of larger size can probably be layered deeper than those of finer size. Shredded pine bark, 1 in. deep, would keep a fabric adequately covered to prevent photodecomposition, yet would not be deep enough to support much weed growth. By contrast, pine bark nuggets or chunks, layered 2 in. to 3 in. deep, would have enough particle overlap to protect the fabric without encouraging much weed growth.

The best combination of landscape fabric and loose mulch in our tests was Weed-X topped with large bark chunks. Weed-X, a nonwoven barrier, has the greatest density of all the fabrics we tested. It's 97% closed, leaving only a 3% risk of weed penetration.

Loose mulches, both inorganic and organic, used in this research project were all applied to a depth of 2 in. When placed atop a landscape fabric, they provided better weed suppression than mulch applied at greater depths.

—*Bonnie Lee Appleton*

There are countless designs for cold frames, but they all share a common aim: to protect the plants inside from inhospitable growing conditions outside. This ready-made, aluminum cold frame with a fiberglass top shelters cool-season vegetables.

Cold Frames

Simple structures with a world of garden uses

by David Wright

A bottomless box with a transparent lid. It doesn't sound like much, but a cold frame can give a gardener something that is always in short supply: time. For centuries farmers and gardeners have used cold frames to trap the warmth of the sun's rays to get a jump on spring and to push the growing season deep into fall and even into winter.

At Missouri Botanical Garden we make extensive, year-round use of our cold frames to harden off bedding plant and vegetable seedlings, to propagate woody plants and perennials, to carry our bonsai collection over winter and to force bulbs for indoor color during the winter. Even with all of the cold frame space we have at our disposal, we never seem to have quite enough to grow all of the things we'd like.

A cold frame creates a protected environment for its resident plants. Like a greenhouse, the cold frame captures and holds solar heat, lifting the internal temperature well above that outside. At the same time, the cold frame's walls provide sanctuary from wintry drafts.

Since a cold frame isn't really cold, its name gives rise to confusion. A cold frame is "cold" only relative to a hotbed, which got its name first. To the casual observer, a cold frame and a hotbed appear to be identical. The only difference is that a hotbed has an internal heat source (traditionally, fermenting horse manure; but today, more often, an electric heating cable). We don't use hotbeds in our operations at Missouri Botanical Garden, but a regulated heat source would certainly add another dimension of usefulness to a cold frame.

The easiest way to acquire a cold frame is to buy one. Various sizes and designs are available from mail-order garden suppliers (see Sources on p. 83) or local garden centers. These ready-made frames are efficient and often portable, but they can be costly, as much as $130 for a basic unit. With a little bit of planning and some rudimentary carpentry skills, you can build your own cold frame. Building one yourself will allow you to size the unit to fit your needs and to save money. Later, I will describe a simple cold frame that you can assemble with ease.

Putting a cold frame to use

Extending the season—The most common use of a cold frame is as a means to stretch the growing season. In early spring, you can get a head start on the vegetable or flower garden by seeding directly into the cold frame cool-season plants such as onions, lettuce, snapdragons and pansies. To get the earliest possible jump on spring, I start the seeds of these flowers and vegetables indoors, when it's still too cold to sow them outdoors, even in a cold frame. Once I've transplanted the seedlings into individual containers, I set them out into the frames to grow to planting size.

All seedlings started indoors, no matter how tolerant they are of cool temperatures, require a period of gradual acclimation to outdoor conditions. Plants rushed out into the garden are often irreversibly overwhelmed by the intensity of the sun, the strength of the breezes and the abrupt change in relative humidity and temperature. A cold frame acts as an excellent halfway house for pampered seedlings. Inside its protective walls, plants accustomed to life indoors receive measured exposure to the elements, making their establishment outdoors much easier. The thousands of bedding plants we grow each year spend at least a week in the cold frames before being planted out.

Many vegetables that tolerate or even prefer the cooler temperatures of early spring also do well in autumn. You can start a fall crop of such vegetables as kale and lettuce in mid- to late summer and put the plants into the cold frame as the cool weather approaches. Inside the frame, these vegetables will continue to yield late into fall and even into winter. (For more on cool season leaf crops, see *FG #15*, p. 26.)

Propagation—Cold frames are useful as aids in propagating plants. For ex-

ample, you can start many trees, shrubs and perennials native to cold-winter regions from seeds sown in a cold frame. These plants often bear seeds that have evolved a protective mechanism which prevents their germination during the winter months. Most such seeds require a 60- to 90-day cold and damp period before germination will occur. You can simulate this cold and damp period by sowing seeds in pots or flats of moist peat moss and placing them in a cold frame in late fall or early winter. The ensuing winter months will provide

the necessary cold temperatures. The frame moderates temperature fluctuations and protects the seeds from foraging rodents. In the spring, the seeds germinate naturally. I have grown many tree and shrub species this way.

Cold frames can also be an aid in propagating woody plants from dormant cuttings. They create an excellent environment for rooting cuttings of needled evergreens and deciduous shrubs taken from late fall through winter. Yews, junipers and arborvitae root well, albeit slowly, under these conditions. You can also root shrubs

The substantial cold frames at the Missouri Botanical Garden are made of poured concrete and glazed with space-age plastic. Author David Wright formerly supervised the year-round use of these frames to harden off seedlings, propagate woody plants and perennials, overwinter plants needing extra protection and force bulbs.

Photo: Tim Ryan, courtesy Missouri Botanical Garden

such as privet, holly and some viburnums by this method.

Overwintering—Here in St. Louis, we usually see the mercury dip to lows of -5°F to -10°F at least once every winter. During such bitter cold snaps, the air inside our cold frames is as much as 20° warmer than the outside air. Perhaps more important, the cold frames moderate abrupt temperature fluctuations, which are often more harmful to plants than the cold alone.

Cold frames are a good place to overwinter young, immature plants, plants in containers and marginally hardy plants that would suffer injury or death if exposed to the full brunt of winter. Insulate the roots with a layer of straw or a similar mulch. Roots are damaged by sub-freezing temperatures that leave the tops unscathed.

At Missouri Botanical Garden, we also overwinter our bonsai plants in cold frames. Many of the plants used in bonsai are native to cold winter regions and therefore need a cool resting period between growing seasons. A cold frame, in conjunction with a heavy mulch, provides the necessary cool period while giving substantial

protection for the plants' roots which are sometimes exposed in shallow pots.

Forcing—During winter, a cold frame is also an ideal environment for forcing spring bulbs. Many such bulbs have a natural cold chilling requirement which must be satisfied before they will bloom. Pot up tulips, daffodils, hyacinths and freesias in the fall, place them in the frame and mulch the containers heavily on all sides to keep the bulbs from freezing. Throughout the winter you can then bring pots of bulbs into the house for

Easy access to the plants, through the basement window as well as through the hinged top, is a feature of this unique redwood cold frame with Plexiglas glazing.

a succession of blooms during the late winter months. At the Garden, we force hundreds of bulbs this way every year.

Building a simple cold frame

There are almost as many possible cold frame designs as there are gardeners. The simplest models employ plywood for the walls and a sheet of plastic for the lid. They are lightweight and portable, but unable to protect plants from the blasts of a harsh winter. The most impressive models are made of concrete poured into forms set deep into the ground to take advantage of the warmth of the earth below. Their sashes contain space-age plastics that boast superior insulation and light-transmission qualities.

The cold frame that I will describe here is solid and durable enough to leave out over winter. (See the construction drawing on the facing page.) Although heavy, it is portable if you can get a friend to help you lift it. You can vary the dimensions to suit your needs and the materials you have on hand. This cold frame is roughly 6 ft. long and 3 ft. wide to match the storm-sash lid. You can use a variety of other widely-available materials, such as sheets of plastic, Plexiglas or fiberglass for the glazing (the transparent lid) of your frame. I have chosen storm sashes because they are already assembled and ready for use.

The frame is 24 in. tall at the back, which allows room for taller plants such as bonsai or newly propagated trees and shrubs. If you are using the frame only to harden off seedlings, you may find that 12 in. to 16 in. is sufficient. The front wall of the frame is 8 in. lower than the back wall. Whatever your design, I recommend a minimum difference of 6 in. to 12 in. The resulting angle maximizes the amount of sunlight entering the frame; it also encourages rain to run off the outside of the sash and condensation to run forward down the interior.

When you put your first market pack of seedlings inside this cold frame, you'll think it's enormous. But my experience suggests that once you start using it, you'll find that you can fill it all too quickly. If you decide to make an even bigger frame, I recommend that you extend the length rather than the width—it's hard to reach the plants at the back of a frame that is more than 3 ft. deep.

When siting the cold frame, choose a location that receives at least six to eight hours of sun and that is protect-

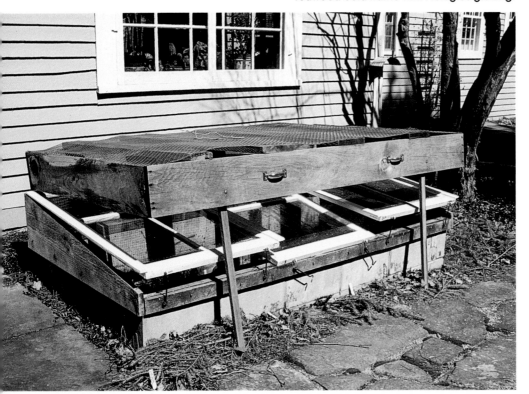

This cold frame is built to protect plants from a harsh winter. The floor of the frame rests several inches below ground level to take advantage of the warmth of the earth. The cinder block walls provide extra insulation from cold drafts. And a hinged frame covered with hardware cloth serves to prevent ice and snow from sliding off of the roof and breaking the storm sash glazing.

Photos: top, Rebecca Schubert; below, staff

ed from strong, direct winds. The south wall of a garage or some other building is ideal. Drainage is also important, particularly if the frame is in use over winter. If the soil below the frame does not drain well, consider excavating 3 in. to 4 in. of soil and replacing it with gravel or sand.

You can construct the frame out of wood, poured concrete, concrete blocks, brick or stone. Wood, though less durable, is the easiest to work with. It provides adequate protection from the elements in most climates, though in colder regions you may want to add polystyrene insulation board to the inside of the frame for additional insulation. Since the frame will be in contact with the ground, I recommend using pressure-treated lumber.

Once you've cut the wood to the appropriate length, assembling the pieces is simple. Fasten the boards with corrosion-resistant screws or nails to 2×4s cut to the height of the wall. Space the 2×4s at 3-ft. to 4-ft. intervals, depending on the length of the frame. Then join the four walls to 2×4s set upright in each corner. Attach the sashes to the back wall of the frame with hinges so that the sashes remain in place when closed, but allow easy access into the frame. Be sure that the sashes fit snugly on the top of the frame and to each other to minimize air and water seepage.

Caring for the plants

On sunny days, a cold frame may do its job too well. Internal temperatures may soar to 80°F or 90°F or more, even though the outside temperature may be hovering around the freezing mark. Even if the heat doesn't kill or damage the plants outright, it may encourage soft growth which can be killed when the temperature drops dramatically at night.

To prevent overheating, it's important to vent the cold frame. Any sort of a prop will do. Notch the prop at 4-in. to 6-in. intervals so you can vary the height of the sash. I recommend that you aim for a maximum daytime temperature of 75°F inside the frame. A thermometer hung on the frame's north wall will allow you to monitor the temperature.

You can purchase temperature-activated vent arms that will automatically open the sash when the temperature climbs above a predetermined point. (See Charley's Greenhouse Supplies and Walt Nicke Company in Sources at right.) Make sure

A Simple Cold Frame

The dimensions of this cold frame were chosen to accommodate three 3-ft.-long × 2-ft.-wide storm sashes. Alter the dimensions to fit the windows you buy. You can increase the size of the frame by using more sashes, or decrease it by using fewer.

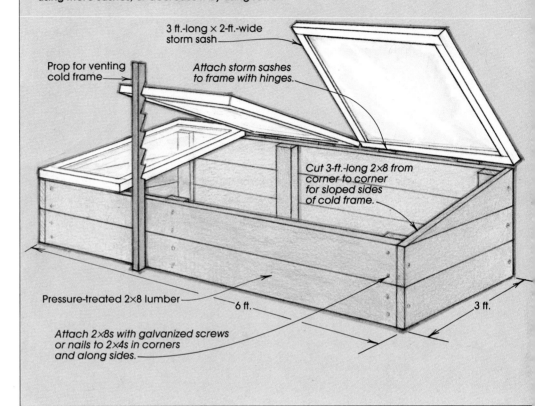

3 ft.-long × 2-ft.-wide storm sash

Prop for venting cold frame

Attach storm sashes to frame with hinges.

Cut 3-ft.-long 2×8 from corner to corner for sloped sides of cold frame.

Pressure-treated 2×8 lumber — 6 ft. — 3 ft.

Attach 2×8s with galvanized screws or nails to 2×4s in corners and along sides.

SOURCES

The following mail-order garden supply companies carry one or more ready-made cold frames. Most are shipped in pieces and will therefore require some assembly.

Bramen Company, Inc., P.O. Box 70, Salem, MA 01970, 508-745-7765. Catalog free.

Charley's Greenhouse Supplies, 1569 Memorial Highway, Mount Vernon, WA 98273, 800-322-4707. Catalog $2.

Growing Naturally, P.O. Box 54, 149 Pine Lane, Pineville, PA 18946, 215-598-7025. Catalog free.

Kinsman Company, Inc., River Road, Point Pleasant, PA 18950, 800-733-5613. Catalog free.

The Walt Nicke Company, 36 McLeod Lane, P.O. Box 433, Topsfield, MA 01983, 508-887-3388. Catalog free.

Park Seed Co., Cokesbury Road, Greenwood, SC 29647-0001, 800-845-3369. Catalog free.

Smith & Hawken, 25 Corte Madera, Mill Valley, CA 94961, 415-383-2000. Catalog free.

that the arm you buy is strong enough to lift your sash.

Plants in a cold frame require frequent watering. The sash prevents them from receiving normal rainfall, and heat trapped by the sash and the breezes allowed in to vent the frame can quickly cause the soil—particularly the soil in containers—to dry out. Check the cold frame frequently, as often as once a day when the sun is out, and water as needed.

As winter approaches, pests may visit your cold frame. Mice and slugs are the two main culprits. For mice, a tight, well-constructed frame is the best deterrent, but mouse bait from the hardware store is good insurance. For slugs, there are a number of effective products available. I find that pelletized baits are the easiest to handle. Shallow containers filled with beer are also effective. □

David Wright is the owner and operator of Wright's Perennial Farms located in Kaukauna, Wisconsin. Wright was formerly in charge of the production greenhouses at the Missouri Botanical Garden.

Stretch the Growing Season

Cold frames let you jump-start spring planting and winter over tender plants

Start the growing season early. By the time the grass turns green in spring, the author has a second batch of flower, herb and vegetable seedlings growing in his cold frame.

by John Mapel

There's nothing like serving freshly harvested lettuce, spinach and radishes to Thanksgiving dinner guests.

I can make such an offering because I start vegetables in my cold frames in late summer for fall harvests. A cold frame is simply a bottomless box covered with glass or clear plastic and heated by the sun. I have three cold frames to extend the growing seasons in spring and summer and to protect tender plants in winter.

My cold frames let me get a head start on gardening in the spring. When it is still too cold to plant in my garden, I start hundreds of flower, herb and vegetable seedlings in frames here in Grafton, Massachusetts (USDA Hardiness Zone 5 [-20°F]). By the last frost date, the seedlings are big enough to set out (see photo, above).

We all have been frustrated by watching a sudden rainstorm wash prized seeds away. But if you sow them in a cold frame, you can protect seeds and seedlings from bad weather by simply shutting the lid.

Growing tasty plants in a cold frame keeps pesky varmints, such as rabbits and raccoons, from beating you to the first summer salad. All you have to do is close the sash at night to shut them out.

I can also save tender ornamentals and herbs from freezing by overwintering them in my cold frames. A closed cold frame that is covered to block out sun (I use evergreen boughs, but any material that prevents light from entering works) creates an insulated, cold environment, which is ideal for dormant plants.

An early start

You can begin the growing season in late winter by starting plants in a cold frame. Early-blooming annuals, including cornflowers (*Centaurea cyanus*), sweet peas (*Lathyrus odoratus*) and stocks (*Matthiola* spp.), as well as cool-weather vegetables, such as cabbage, spinach and peas, will germinate in a cold frame in late February or early March—even when nighttime temperatures outdoors drop below freezing.

Just keep handy an insulating cover, such as an old blanket or water-repellent tarp (see photo at right). Cover the sash before sundown each evening to trap and hold in the collected solar heat during the night. Then uncover the frame each morning.

Plants started early mature early. If you usually plant seeds in your garden on April 1, you can sow them in your cold frame on March 1. But if you sow the same seeds two months early, don't expect to harvest a crop two months early—usually a month's lead time is all you will gain.

Extend the growing season

I harvest vegetables well into December. I plant lettuce; peas; radishes; and herbs, such as parsley and rosemary (*Rosmarinus officinalis*), in a cold frame in late summer. They mature before freezing weather, and I

winter them over until I am ready to harvest them.

Cold frames are also ideal for wintering over semihardy ornamentals, such as chrysanthemums; for storing bulbs to force for early spring flowers (for more information, see "Forcing Bulbs," *FG* #34, pp. 36–39); and for overwintering hardwood cuttings. Hardwood cuttings are cuttings taken from the stems of dormant woody

Siting a cold frame
In autumn the sun is in the southern sky. The best exposure for a cold frame is a south-facing exposure so that it can fully absorb the warmth of the sun, making it possible to continue growing plants as outdoor temperatures cool. The cold-frame lid, or sash, should slope gradually downward from the hinges at the back of the frame to the front so that it can face the sun's rays.

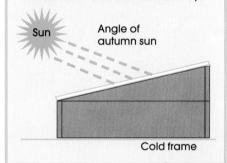

Sun

Angle of autumn sun

Cold frame

plants. These cuttings need to be stored in cool, moist conditions (burying them in damp sand in a cold frame over winter is ideal) until spring, when they can be planted out.

Any cold-frame plants that you want to winter over must go through a hardening-off period, just like their outdoor cousins, to prepare them for dormancy. In the fall, prop the sash open far enough to prevent heat from building up inside the frame. When the outside temperatures stabilize at just below freezing, close the sash and cover it to keep out light. Don't water or fertilize dormant plants, but do peek in on them occasionally to head off problems, such as nesting mice.

Cold-frame culture

Starting plants in a cold frame differs little from propagating and growing plants in the garden. (For information on starting seeds, see "Annuals from seeds," *FG* #36, p. 48.)

First, decide whether you want to grow the plants directly in soil inside the frame, in pots or in cell packs (compartmentalized planting trays). I prefer cell packs because plants can be easily removed from the flexible cells

Bundle up at night. You can start seeds in late winter in a cold frame. Just cover the sash before sundown with an old blanket or tarp to trap heat inside overnight.

and because root damage and transplant shock are minimized. I simply set the cell packs in trays directly on the floor of the cold frame. Treat individual pots the same way.

If you decide to sow seeds directly in the frame, however, you should put down a 3- or 4-in. layer of gravel as a base, then top it with the same thickness of commercial potting soil, which is better than garden soil for sowing seeds because it is free of weed seeds and diseases.

Different plants require different temperatures for optimum growth. Tomatoes, peppers and squash, for instance, are warm-season crops. Their seeds and those of tender flowering plants, such as nicotianas and marigolds, require warm temperatures in order to germinate. Here's where having more than one cold frame comes in handy—have one to start cool season crops, and another to start warm-season crops.

To prepare a cold frame for starting warmth-loving seeds or plants, I temporarily bury a soil-heating cable (available at garden centers) under a 2- or 3-in.-thick layer of sand. I cover the sand with wire mesh to protect the cable when I dig in the frame. Then I connect the heating cable to a weatherproof extension cord, plug it

in and set flats of cell packs directly on the wire mesh. The heating cable keeps the soil in the cubes at about 70°F. If you choose to sow seeds in a bed warmed by a cable, simply cover the wire mesh with potting soil, 3 or 4 in. deep, and proceed as directed above, keeping the cable plugged in only until the seeds have germinated and are off to a good start.

Avoiding disease

You can minimize the risk of diseases such as damping-off, which thrives in moist, stuffy conditions, by properly watering and ventilating your cold frame. (For more information, see "Disease-Free Seedlings," *FG* #30, pp. 12–14.) Water early in the day to allow time for moisture to evaporate from plants and the soil's surface before evening. Ventilate the cold frame by lifting the sash when temperatures inside reach 70°F. Cleaning cold frames also discourages disease, so remove weeds and unhealthy or dead leaves and plants.

Siting and temperature control

The best exposure for a cold frame is a southern one because it faces the warming rays of the autumn sun, which will prolong your growing season. (An eastern exposure is second best.) The sash should slope gradually downward from the hinges at the back of the frame to the front so that it can directly face the sun's rays (see illustration on p. 85).

An ideal temperature range for growing many kinds of plants is between a daytime high of 70°F and a nighttime low of 45°F. On a sunny, cloudless day, however, temperatures can soar well over 100°F inside a closed cold frame. During the growing season, when the temperature in a cold frame reaches 70°F, prop the sash open to ventilate the frame sufficiently so that it can maintain optimal temperatures.

To warm up a cold frame on overcast or cloudy days during the growing season, keep the sash lowered or completely closed, to trap heat inside and hold it there throughout the night.

If you set the cold frame 6 to 8 in. below the soil's surface, stored heat

Building a cold frame

A cold frame is just a box, usually made of wood. A hinged lid (sash) covered with glass or plastic allows light to pass inside where plants grow. Cold frames should be sunk into the ground and be airtight when closed to insulate plants inside against fluctuating ground and air temperatures. To regulate the ventilation and temperature inside the frame, the glass or plastic sash should be attached by removable (loose-pin) hinges so that it can be raised, lowered or removed as needed.

You can purchase ready-made cold frames from some garden-supply catalogs and garden centers, or you can make your own. (For more information on building or purchasing cold frames, see "Cold Frames," pp. 80-83.) Cold frames can be made of scrap lumber or exterior-grade plywood in any size or shape that suits you. (Measure the flats or containers you plan to put in it and choose dimensions accordingly.) But I make mine from rot-resistant, pressure-treated 2 x 8s because there is no waste. (For details, see photos at right).

I cut six lengths of board to make a 4-ft.-square cold frame that is about 16 in. deep (see bottom photo, near right). A frame this deep is adequate for starting seeds in spring, growing crops for fall harvests and wintering over many plants. But I made one frame three boards (nearly 2 ft.) deep. This frame is deep enough for me to overwinter even tender herbs without subjecting them to the killing freezes that occur here in Massachusetts.

—J.M.

from the sun will radiate upward through the soil at night and help to warm the interior.

In the coldest growing weather, a 100-watt incandescent light bulb plugged into a weatherproof extension cord and hung in the cold frame can keep the temperature inside above freezing.

You can predict when to ventilate and when to cover the cold frame if

Keep seedlings snug
An electric soil-heating cable keeps warmth-loving seedlings at constant room temperature. The author lays heating cable under a bed of sand covered with wire mesh. Cell pack flats sit directly on the wire mesh.

Sand, 2 or 3 in. deep

Wire mesh

Heating cable

Build a simple box. Six lengths of 2 x 8s make up this cold frame. Braces, or cleats, of 1 x 3s are nailed to the outside walls of the frame. (I used to fasten them to interior walls, but nailing them outside, as shown here, provides more growing area within.) Cutting one board in half diagonally provides just the right slant to allow the lid (sash) of the frame to be two boards high at the back, sloping down to one board high at the front of the frame. Caulk cracks between boards to seal out freezing winter air.

A removable sash affords ventilation. Make the sash from 2 x 4 boards cut to fit the frame. Cover it with wire mesh and plastic film. Fasten the sash to the frame with weather-resistant, galvanized, loose-pin hinges (available at hardware stores) so that it can be removed in hot weather for ventilation.

Screws make sturdy joints. The author, right, and a friend fasten the corners of the cold frame together with galvanized deck screws.

you know how temperatures inside are affected by the weather. To track temperatures, place a thermometer that records high and low temperatures (available at garden centers) or an ordinary outdoor thermometer inside the cold frame. Then record high and low temperatures inside the frame until you are able to establish a pattern for ventilating based on predicted outdoor temperatures.

If manually adjusting the sash is inconvenient, you can purchase a device that automatically opens and closes the sash when the air inside reaches a selected temperature. (For more information, see "Cold Frames," pp. 80-83.) These heat-activated vent regulators have one drawback—they can't raise heavy sashes; they are more suitable for lifting plastic-covered sashes than glass ones.

During the warmest months, remove the sash and replace it with a ventilated frame covered with anything that will reduce the light entering by 40 or 50 percent. I make covers from lattice, snow fence, old window screens and even burlap bags. □

John Mapel is a horticulturist at Tower Hill Botanic Garden in Boylston, Massachusetts.

Indoor Sunlight

How to grow plants with electric lights

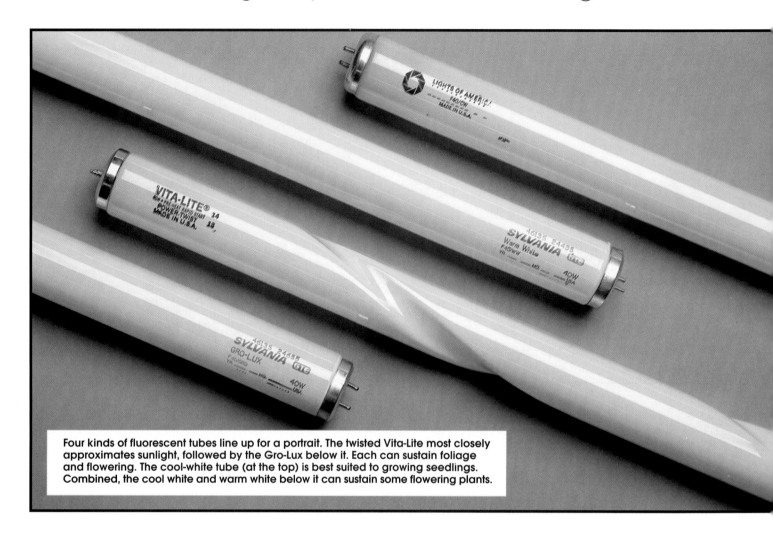

Four kinds of fluorescent tubes line up for a portrait. The twisted Vita-Lite most closely approximates sunlight, followed by the Gro-Lux below it. Each can sustain foliage and flowering. The cool-white tube (at the top) is best suited to growing seedlings. Combined, the cool white and warm white below it can sustain some flowering plants.

by Charles C. Powell

Growing plants indoors under electric lights is a sleight-of-hand trick. Imperfect substitutes for the energy of the sun, electric lights are limited in intensity and in wavelengths (colors of the spectrum). To grow plants indoors, you must understand how electric lights differ from sunlight and then compensate.

Plants need light for photosynthesis—the conversion of light first into chemical energy and then into carbohydrates, which the plants use for growth and flowering. Sunlight supplies growing plants with the intensity, day length (photoperiod) and wavelengths they need for photosynthesis. When you grow plants under lights, you cannot match the intensity and wavelength of sunlight, but you can get good results by choosing the right lights, placing them a suitable distance from the plants and controlling the photoperiod.

The light plants need

Intensity is the amount of light a source provides. It's measured in "footcandles" (the amount of light an "international candle" casts over a 1-sq. ft. surface area from 1 ft. away).

The sun is more intense than any electric light. A sunny garden in summer receives 10,000 to 15,000 footcandles of light, and a shady summer garden receives from 4,000 to 8,000 footcandles. By comparison, two typical 40-watt fluorescent tubes deliver only 50 to 800 footcandles, depending on how close to the tubes the plant is placed. For instance, at a distance of 1 in. to 3 in. from fluorescent tubes, the light intensity is about 800 footcandles, while at 12 in. from the tubes it falls to about 250 footcandles. (See drawing on the facing page.)

Because electric lights are less intense than sunlight, a plant needs more hours of daily exposure to electric lights than it would to sunlight. For example, a fig tree (*Ficus benjamina*), needs

2400 "footcandle hours" of light per day. If a lamp provides 150 footcandles, the plant would need 16 hours of exposure each day (2400 ÷ 150 = 16). With a stronger lamp, the photoperiod would shrink. For example, you can provide the same light level by exposing the plant to 300 footcandles for eight hours (2400 ÷ 300 = 8). You can also adjust the footcandles a plant receives by altering the distance to the light.

Most plants need at least eight hours under lights to sustain photosynthesis when they're grown indoors. Seedlings need at least 750 footcandles of electric light during their daily eight-hour photoperiod, so you must place them 1-in. to 3-in. from fluorescent tubes for eight hours. [A list of plants and their footcandle requirements appears in *The Healthy Indoor Plant* by the author and Rosemarie Rossetti, Rosewell Publishing, Inc., P.O. Box 2920, Columbus, OH 43216; $29.50 ppd.]

For many plants, photoperiod is just as important as the total amount of light they need. These plants need certain photoperiods to grow well, to initiate flowering or to enter dormancy. Summer-blooming annuals, for example, often require long photoperiods to initiate flowering. For these plants, a high intensity of light for less than eight hours per day would be inadequate, even if the total footcandle hours were "correct." Other plants, such as autumn-flowering chrysanthemums and poinsettias, are short-day bloomers,

requiring light for eight hours or less per day during bloom periods to begin flowering. Tuberous begonias, by contrast, are long-day bloomers that require short days after flowering to initiate dormancy. [For a list of plants and their day length requirements see *Rodale's Encyclopedia of Indoor Gardening*, edited by Anne M. Halpin, Rodale Press, Emmaus, Pennsylvania, 1980.]

One final quality of light also affects how plants grow—the combination of wavelengths. For plants, sunlight offers the ideal combination—strong in blue and red wavelengths, which plants need to photosynthesize efficiently. Neither blue nor red is sufficient alone. Red light promotes flowering, but red light alone produces tall, spindly growth. Blue light promotes compact growth with dark green leaves, but blue light alone produces few flowers. Most electric lights are deficient in blue or red. To compensate, you have to extend the photoperiod or raise the intensity.

A choice of lights

Let's look at the range of lights that are capable of sustaining plants. They are not equally suitable for indoor growing. You'll want to select those that provide wavelengths needed by plants at intensities low enough for you to live with. For example, high-intensity lamps, which are often used to light outdoor areas at night, are poor choices for growing plants indoors. Although

they provide ample blue wavelengths, they're too bright to look at. The familiar household light bulbs are equally poor choices—they comfortably illuminate living areas, but they are deficient in blue wavelengths.

High-pressure sodium lamps—These high-intensity lights provide the blue wavelengths needed to promote sturdy stems, side shoots and leaves on plants. They are very bright, however, with about 300 footcandles of light reaching a bench of plants from ceiling-mounted lamps, and so are best used at night or in unfrequented areas of the house. They can be purchased from lighting specialists, are expensive ($100-$300) and require professional installation.

Metal-halide lamps—These powerful lamps emit the wavelengths that plants need at a high intensity. Lamps placed in the ceiling provide 300 footcandles of light per square foot over a wide area. They are less expensive ($40-$120) than sodium lamps and cost less to operate, but they also must be professionally installed.

Fluorescent lamps—These lamps are the most available, affordable and widely used lights for growing plants. There are several kinds of fluorescent tubes, and each emits a different spectrum. One type, called cool white, is rich in blue wavelengths and weak in red wavelengths. Another type, called warm white, is rich in red wavelengths, but weak in blue wavelengths. Combining one of each in a two-tube fixture provides a spectrum that will give many plants the light they need to grow and flower. You can also buy a wide-spectrum or full-spectrum fluorescent tube that emits the right combination of wavelengths for plants. These "grow lights" match up to 90% of sunlight's spectrum; regular fluorescents match only about 50%.

Fluorescent tubes vary greatly in cost and longevity. Cool-white, 4-ft. long tubes cost as little as $1, while full-spectrum, 4-ft. long tubes can cost $15 (but last up to three times longer).

Different types of fluorescent tubes are suited to different growing purposes. Cool-white lamps are sufficient for starting seeds. A combination of cool whites and warm whites is good for growing seedlings, houseplants and easy-to-bloom plants such as African violets. Two wide-spectrum or full-spectrum fluorescents provide even

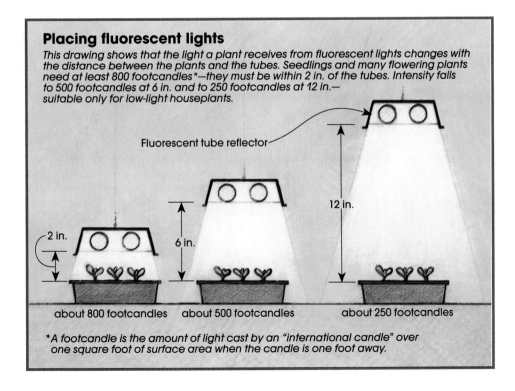

Placing fluorescent lights

This drawing shows that the light a plant receives from fluorescent lights changes with the distance between the plants and the tubes. Seedlings and many flowering plants need at least 800 footcandles*—they must be within 2 in. of the tubes. Intensity falls to 500 footcandles at 6 in. and to 250 footcandles at 12 in.— suitable only for low-light houseplants.

Fluorescent tube reflector

12 in.

2 in.

6 in.

about 800 footcandles   about 500 footcandles   about 250 footcandles

*A footcandle is the amount of light cast by an "international candle" over one square foot of surface area when the candle is one foot away.

more usable wavelengths for growth and flowering than a cool-white and a warm-white tube combined.

To use fluorescent lamps efficiently, you must direct as much light as possible from the tube to the plant, so the fixture should have an overhead, white-painted reflector with side baffles, like those that come with shop lights. A pair of 40-watt, 4-ft. long, cool-white fluorescent lights, commonly sold with a shop light (a two-tube fixture with a reflective metal hood) for about $10 at hardware and discount stores, will light a growing area of about 2 ft. by 4 ft. (For more information see "$10 lights for indoor plants" at right.)

Where you put plants makes a difference with fluorescent lamps. Light is most intense at the center of a fluorescent tube, so place plants that need higher intensity light—flowering plants, cacti and vegetable plants—under the center of the lamp. Put seedlings, cuttings and foliage plants at the ends of the tubes.

Whether using high intensity lamps or fluorescent tubes, you have to adjust for changing intensities. The intensity of light provided by fluorescent tubes dwindles with age, falling by about one half after six months, and gradually thereafter. Watch plants growing under aging lamps for legginess—long, spindly stems are a sign of weakening light. Lengthen photoperiods accordingly or shorten the distance between plants and lamps to maintain intensity. Replace weakening fluorescent tubes when black rings appear at the ends. When you install new lamps, appropriately shorten photoperiods and remember to raise the fixture if you had lowered it. Regularly wipe away dust, which reduces light.

Whatever type of lights you use, you must turn them on and off each day for a constant photoperiod. You can do it manually, but it's easier to use plug-in electric timer units. They cost $7 to $20 from hardware stores or mail-order catalogs. You simply set a rotary dial to the times you want to turn the lights on and off, or program exposure times into the keypad of an electronic timer, and plug the timer into an outlet, then plug the light into the timer. Your plants will have an ideal day. □

Charles C. Powell is a professor at Ohio State University, Columbus, Ohio.

The pink plumes of celosia and the pink and purple flowers of alyssum bloom in cell packs below a fluorescent fixture. Seedlings can get a good start under fluorescents.

$10 lights for indoor plants

by Larry Porter

I grow plants indoors with the simplest of setups—ordinary fluorescent shop lights (4-ft. fluorescent tubes in fixtures with white reflectors) and a timer. In Billings, Montana, where I garden, the growing season is three months long from spring to fall. Shop lights let me enjoy blooming plants during our long, cold winters.

Common 4-ft. long shop lights are sold by all hardware stores for about $10 and are easy to install. I simply attach chains to the shop lights and hang them from ceiling hooks. This arrangement lets me raise or lower the shop lights by putting a different chain link over the hook. However you hang shop lights, allow several inches of ventilation space above the fixture when it is fully raised to dissipate the heat produced by the tubes.

If you use lights, as I do, in a damp and stuffy basement, you'll have to observe two precautions. First, use an outdoor extension cord, which is designed for damp conditions. Second, provide air circulation to protect plants against fungal diseases. A window fan will do—set it on low and put it in a dry place off the floor.

Shop lights come with two cool-white tubes, but I customized my setup by replacing one tube with a grow-light. Cool-white fluorescent lamps are adequate for growing foliage plants and seedlings, but not for growing many flowering plants. Grow lights provide the wavelengths of light plants need to flower as well as to grow. You can also use one cool white tube and one warm white tube, which is less costly than a grow light, but has almost the same effect.

I've devised a test to see if my plants are receiving enough light to grow well. With the shop light turned on, I hold my hand directly under the tubes. If I see a faint shadow from my hand on the foliage below, I know that the shop light is giving off enough light to grow most plants.

After plants spend a couple of months under lights, their appearance signals whether they're receiving the correct amount of light. If the plants are tall and spindly, the light is inadequate, and I lower the shop light. If they're shorter than average with leaves that curve downward away from the light, the light is too intense, and so I raise the shop light.

Anybody can find enough space for a shop light. I've hung them in my basement, in my garage and over a shelf above the kitchen sink. I've even put them in my greenhouse to lengthen our short, Montana winter days.

Larry Porter gardens under shop lights in Billings, Montana.

Window Boxes

In early summer, this window box is overflowing with pansies and white lobelias.

Few gardens are as manageable or as much fun as those grown in a box beneath a window. No property is too small, no plant too humble and no gardener too busy for a window box. Some folks treat a box like a tiny border. Growing plants from seeds or cuttings, they'll experiment with combinations of foliage, flower, texture and form, changing them with the seasons or even more frequently. Others buy potted annuals at the local nursery and redo the box when the mood strikes or the plants get ratty. Done with imagination, either method can produce stunning results.

Window boxes can be made of all sorts of materials—stone, clay, plastic, hypertufa—but wood seems most popular. Take five boards, a handful of galvanized nails and some shelf brackets, and in half an hour you'll be in business. Coated with paint or lined with a rigid plastic shell from a garden center, the box will last longer than if you let the elements create a "rustic" look.

Window-box gardening is not complicated, but there are a few important considerations. First, a box full of wet soil is heavy, so gauge your fastenings accordingly. Second, drainage is as crucial for plants in a window box as it is for those in any other container, so be sure to provide drainage holes. Third, soil in a window box can dry out quickly, particularly in full sun. When you choose your window, remember that you'll want to get at the box easily for regular watering.

Many plants can be grown in window boxes. There's no reason why you can't grow perennials in a box—hardy herbs, sempervivums and similar small plants come to mind. But one of the pleasures of window-box gardening is changing the display several times a year, and for this annuals make most sense. Putting in the plants is generally less of a problem than taking them out. No one likes to uproot perfectly healthy plants. But when plants are past their prime, it's time to make a fresh start.

The most important ingredient in window-box gardening is imagination. To inspire your creativity, we offer the photos on these three pages, taken by Solomon Skolnick on his travels up and down the East Coast and in England for *The Window Box Book*. In addition to many more of Skolnick's photos, the book contains information from Anne Halpin on window-box design, gardening techniques and styles. *The Window Box Book* was published last year by Simon and Schuster at $14.95.

Above: Two terra-cotta planter boxes hold yellow violas, red petunias (on the left) and deep-pink Martha Washington geraniums (on the right), and green-and-white variegated English ivy.

Left: An evergreen gold-spot aucuba is the centerpiece here. Red geraniums, pink impatiens, and red-and-white petunias rise to either side, while purple lobelia trails over the front.

Below: Trailing swags of English ivy, tropical-looking large-leaved aralias, and dozens of flowering geraniums, lobelias and petunias turn the facade of this London pub into a vertical garden.

Above: Here's a soft-colored combination that would thrive in an eastern exposure—lavender and purple lobelias, pale- and rosy-pink impatiens, pink-and-white fuchsias, and variegated English ivy. Densely planted window boxes like this one dry out quickly, and usually need daily watering.
Right: Variegated English ivy and ivy-leaf geraniums make a low-maintenance combination that looks attractive from planting time until hard frost. These plants can tolerate full sun.
Below: Two purple lobelias, a white alyssum and a red begonia fill a nook in a brick wall.

Index

The 22 articles in this book originally appeared in *Fine Gardening* magazine.
The date of first publication, issue number and page numbers for each article are given below.